VOTE YOUR CONSCIENCE

Party Must Not Trump Principles

Brian Kaylor

Union Mound Publishing

Jefferson City, MO

VOTE YOUR CONSCIENCE
Copyright © 2016 Brian Kaylor

All rights reserved. No part of this book may be reproduced, distributed, or transmitted in any form or by any electronic or mechanical means, without written permission from the publisher, except in the case of brief quotations embodied in critical reviews.

All photos by Brian Kaylor unless otherwise noted.

ISBN-10: 1-945870-01-X
ISBN-13: 978-1-945870-01-9

For John and Ronda. Thanks for your encouragement and inspiration.

Table of Contents

Chapter 1: On a Different Team 1

Chapter 2: A Moral Dilemma 25

Chapter 3: Don't Sell Ya Soul 79

Chapter 4: Victory in Jesus? 111

Chapter 5: I Pledge Allegiance 129

Chapter 6: What Shall We Do? 151

Appendix 1: Casting My Vote (All Day) 175

Appendix 2: Rejecting a 'Loser' Savior 179

Appendix 3: An Eye for an Eye Makes the Bible Blind 183

Appendix 4: On the Jericho ... No, Wait ... Büdingen Road 187

Appendix 5: Fellow Citizens of God's Kingdom 191

Appendix 6: Aylan Kurdi 195

Appendix 7: What Would Jesus of Valdosta Say to Donald Trump . 199

About the Author 205

Acknowledgments 207

Endnotes 209

Chapter 1: On a Different Team

"You're either on the team, or you're not on the team."

It's a line that's echoed down through the ages. Join the team of the powerful or face the consequences. Regardless what you may think of a leader, you fall in line like an obedient kindergartener. If you don't, when the ruler starts passing out privileges you could be left on the sidelines like the odd kid chosen last—if at all—for the recess kickball games. Or worse, you could be on the ruler's blacklist of people to punish. The world includes only winners and losers so if you're not a winner you should at least hang out with them to avoid the label of "loser." This is the call of the world: join the team or else!

The demand to join the team plays out in numerous biblical stories. Throwing spears, King Saul turned mad as he demanded this of David and his allies. Prepping a fiery furnace, King Nebuchadnezzar burned with anger as he demanded this of Shadrach, Meshach, and Abednego. Building a pit of hungry lions, King Darius demanded this of Daniel. Rigging the judicial process, King Ahab and Queen Jezebel greened with envy as they demanded this of Naboth. Wielding a sword,

VOTE YOUR CONSCIENCE

Tetrarch Herod's head swirled with lust as he demanded this of John the baptizer.

> *"You're either on the team, or you're not on the team."*

This is the demand of the powerful. It runs counter to the teachings of Jesus, the sacrificial servant King who offered himself to die rather than demanding his people die for him. For followers of Jesus, the 'my way or the highway' argument shouldn't work too well. We're surrounded by a cloud of witnesses who stood strong for righteousness over rulers, for principles over parties, for conscience over candidates. We are called to avoid the temptations of power. We're called to avoid joining the team just because it's the winning side. We're called to stand on the margins, prophetically proclaiming the truth. The tests will often be smaller and the consequences much less harsh than what the prophets of old faced—or what Christians in other nations face today—but that doesn't excuse compromising.

Preacher-turned-politician Mike Huckabee should know that. For years he served as a Baptist pastor and even as president of the Arkansas Baptist State Convention. Huckabee also wrote numerous books about the importance of character and values in public life. *Character makes a difference*, he preached. Then came the 2016 presidential campaign. In his longshot bid for the Republican nomination, Huckabee at times flirted with the campaign of business mogul Donald Trump. After dropping out—via a tweet on the night of the first actual votes in Iowa—Huckabee defended Trump on several occasions even as he withheld endorsing any remaining candidate. (Huckabee's daughter, who had served as his 2016 campaign manager, went to work for the Trump campaign after her father dropped out.) Huckabee's defense of Trump escalated quickly once Trump became the presumptive nominee following the withdrawal of all other Republican candidates.

"When we nominated various people over the past several election cycles to be president, there were many of us that had some heartburn about particular things over those candidates, but, you know what, we sucked it up and we went out there and we vigorously supported our nominee," Huckabee said on Fox News's *America's Newsroom* on May 5, the morning after Trump's ascension to nominee. "This isn't Burger King. This is an election. And you don't get it all the time just like you want it."[1]

Huckabee said he remains "disappointed" and "outraged" at Republicans unwilling to support Trump and urged them to back the nominee or quit the GOP. Huckabee added, "You're either on the team, or you're not on the team."[2] I used to have great respect for Huckabee.

I even voted for him in the 2008 Republican presidential primary and attended his Iowa caucus victory rally (and then Barack Obama's victory rally that night). Huckabee brought a hopeful message that year that included the need for compassion and cooperation. By the time the 2016 campaign rolled around, he sounded more like a radio talk show host (which he had become) and I cringed often when listening to him. His full-throated endorsement of Trump completed the transformation.

Placing party faithfulness above conscience and principles, Huckabee painted a harsh binary of Republicans versus Democrats where nothing matters except winning positions of power. Apparently character doesn't make a difference, after all. Ironically, even as he chastised fellow Republicans who argued they could not in good conscience endorse a person like Trump, Huckabee lit up with a giddy smile as he praised Trump for being "wise to follow his own heart and conscience." That's an interesting phrase for a former preacher. The Bible speaks of God choosing David as one after God's "own heart," not his own. God told Moses to urge the Hebrew people to obey God's commands "and not prostitute yourselves by chasing after the lusts of your own hearts and eyes."[3] And in Proverbs we are warned, "He who trusts in his own heart is a fool, but he who walks wisely will be delivered"[4] (and that chapter in Proverbs also offers blistering condemnation of people who seek wealth, are wealthy through corruption, are arrogant, and don't give to the poor).

Despite Huckabee's call, some prominent Republicans refuse to join the team (and also refuse to quit the Republican Party). These individuals include former Massachusetts Governor Mitt Romney (the GOP's 2012 presidential nominee), Ohio Governor John Kasich, Senator Ted Cruz of Texas, Senator Ben Sasse of Nebraska, Maryland Governor Larry Hogan, Senator Jeff Flake of Arizona, and former U.S. Presidents George H. W. Bush and George W. Bush. A few Republican politicians have even said they'll vote for Democratic nominee Hillary Clinton! Some supporters of Senator Bernie Sanders—like Cornell West—have said they won't support Clinton or Trump.

Such intraparty opposition is unusually high this year, but not unprecedented. Some Republicans refused to support their party's 1964 nominee, Barry Goldwater, due to his opposition to the 1964 Civil Rights Act and concerns his aggressive foreign policy ideals would spark a nuclear war. Many of those dissenting Republicans—like Michigan Governor and future Republican presidential hopeful George Romney (father of Mitt) stayed in the Republican Party even as they rejected their nominee. They placed principles over party for the election, hoping to steer the party back in future campaigns. Similarly, many Southern Democrats walked out of their party's nominating convention in Philadelphia in 1948 and launched a third-party campaign at a nominating convention in Birmingham a few days later. Although their cause—maintaining segregation—remains morally wrong, they proved themselves willing to put their strongly-held principles ahead of the interests of their own party.

Other efforts to oppose a nominee on principles litter U.S. electoral history. Many of these alternative campaigns barely registered on the electoral scene and left little legacy besides hiding as an answer to a trivia game. Such efforts appear foolish to those who kneel before the altar of political expediency and access. Yet, Jesus warned us that winning is not everything (and definitely not the only thing): "For what will it profit them to gain the whole world and forfeit their life?"[5] It turns out, Jesus wasn't good about joining the team when those in power demanded it. That's exactly how he wound up on a cross.

A Time for Choosing

Less than ten percent of registered voters in the U.S. voted for Trump during the primary process—and the same is true for Democrat Hillary Clinton. You can pick just about any random, crazy conspiracy theory and find that many Americans who believe it. To suggest that we *must* support a candidate just because a few primary voters picked him or her is dangerous rhetoric. It suggests morality is truly up for a few primary voters to pick. We must not surrender our consciences simply because of how a few voters cast their ballots. Consider the case of David Duke. He's the former KKK leader who ran for the Democratic presidential nomination in 1988 and the Republican presidential nomination in 1992, served as a Republican in the Louisiana House of Representatives, enthusiastically backs Trump, and is now running for the U.S. Senate. If Duke had won a presidential nomination, would people have had to join the team? If he wins the GOP nomination for Senate this year, will Republican leaders back him because the voters have spoken? Some GOP leaders already say they will not support Duke if he wins, which means they don't actually join the team every time.

The 'logic' used by Huckabee and others means they must back even Duke as a nominee. If you are willing to draw a line there and say you couldn't support an unrepentant racist, then that means there is, in fact, a line. If there is *any* candidate that you would not support even if your preferred party nominated them, then you've already rejected the 'join the team' argument. Each candidate must then be judged on an individual basis. If you're not willing to be a good team player, that's okay. As chapter 11 of Hebrews shows, you're in good company! It turns out that as Christians we're on a different team first. We do not owe our chief loyalty to the Republican Party or the Democratic Party. Our devotion is not to conservative causes and politicians or liberal causes and politicians. Our allegiance is to the Kingdom of God. We don't follow the elephant or the donkey; we follow the lamb.

I come at this election with a great interest in the religious and political issues at stake. My M.A. and Ph.D. are in political communication. My doctoral dissertation, which won awards from the University of Missouri and the Religious Communication Association, explored religious rhetoric in presidential campaigns from 1976-2008. In it, I examined over 6,000 speeches, debates, and ads to see how our presidential candidates use (and misuse) faith, prayer, and the Bible. A version of that was later published as my second book[6] and won awards from the Religion Communicators Council, the National Communication Association's Political Communication Division, and the Carl Couch Center for Social & Internet Research at the University of Iowa. I taught political communication and advocacy studies at James Madison University and have reported as a journalist on several presidential campaign rallies, conventions, and gatherings. My love of politics goes back to watching elections as a child. I even served as president of my high school's Republican club.

However, my primary passion undergirding this present book comes from my ministry vision. I work for a statewide Baptist network in Missouri, serve several other Baptist organizations in various roles, and previously served as a pastor. I recognize that when we are dealing with issues of religion and politics, the realm of religion has much more to lose. It's like how Baptist professor and author Tony Campolo put it, "Mixing the church and state is like mixing ice cream with cow manure. It may not do much to the manure, but it sure messes up the ice cream."[7] I'm more concerned about what the ice cream has to lose than what the manure does. That is why when Roger Williams, the founder of the first Baptist church in the Americas and the founder of Rhode Island, argued we need a "hedge" or "wall of separation" to protect the "garden" (the church) from the "wilderness" (the state). Thomas Jefferson utilized this metaphor when he wrote to Baptists in Connecticut promising to keep "a wall of separation between Church & State."[8] Showing that pandering is not a new political invention, Jefferson used that language because he knew those Baptists would appreciate it. Pastors engaging in a political campaign isn't the same as church-state mixing (as we'll explore in chapter four), but the clear focus in the rhetoric of Campolo and Williams is the importance of protecting the faithful witness of the church from being perverted. Even in areas outside of church-state mixing, we as Christians can still mess up our ice cream. Or to use a biblical metaphor, we can sell our birthright for a bowl of red (or blue) stew.

This book stands as a call to Christians to avoid the temptation of allowing partisan politics to trump prayerful principles. Many are already failing the test in the 2016 presidential campaign. During the primary season, some Christian leaders offered their blessing to Trump over his opponents. These individuals included Jerry Falwell, Jr. (president of Liberty University), Robert Jeffress (pastor of First Baptist Church of Dallas), Phyllis Schlafly (founder of the Eagle Forum), and "prosperity gospel" televangelists like Mark Burns, Mike Murdock and Paula White.

Once Trump garnered the nomination, many others started to fall in line and join the team by offering their support for a thrice-married casino mogul with mob ties. I'm going to name many of them because we must remember after November who allowed party to trump principles. Among those quickly jumping aboard: David Barton (a pseudo-historian widely consulted in conservative religious-political circles), Marjorie Dannenfelser (head of the Susan B. Anthony List),

Wayne Grudem (seminary professor and author), televangelist John Hagee, Andrea Lafferty (executive director of the now ironically-named Traditional Values Coalition), Richard Land (president of Southern Evangelical Seminary), David Lane (an influential Christian political organizer), Jim Garlow (pastor and author), Anne Graham Lotz (evangelist and author), Eric Metaxas (author and radio host), Ralph Reed (leader of the Faith & Freedom Coalition and former Christian Coalition leader), James Robison (a televangelist who helped connect presidential candidate Ronald Reagan with the evangelical movement), and many church pastors.

In addition to Huckabee, failed 2016 GOP presidential candidates Ben Carson and Rick Santorum also endorsed Trump despite building their careers on preaching the need for character and values in politics. Many more pastors and Christian leaders will likely signal their public support for Trump before election day. Like Huckabee, many of the pastors endorsing Trump previously criticized President Bill Clinton for his sexual sins. Yet, they now embrace someone whose behavior is even worse. If character mattered for Bill Clinton, then it also matters for the guy running against Bill's wife.

Fortunately, some Christian leaders have stood strong in their prophetic critiques of Trump, including Thabiti Anyabwile (pastor in

Washington, D.C.), Denny Burk (professor at Boyce College, a Southern Baptist school), Robert George (author and professor at Princeton University), Max Lucado (author and pastor in Texas), and Russell Moore (president of the Southern Baptist Convention's Ethics & Religious Liberty Commission).

Interestingly, many pastors and Christian leaders who endorsed Ted Cruz during the primaries then threw their support behind Trump after Cruz dropped out. Yet, Cruz refused to endorse, as did John Kasich, Jeb! Bush, and some other Republicans who saw backing Trump as crossing a moral line. Cruz even refused to endorse Trump during a primetime speech at the Republican convention! During that speech, Cruz urged people to "vote your conscience," which led Trump supporters to fill the arena with boos. If you're booing a call to conscience, that says something about what you know about your candidate. As booing continued, Cruz kept talking about the importance of principles. He then walked off the stage without bowing to party demands, which should particularly shame those who quickly caved to Trump. Cruz, a member of the Republican caucus in the United States Senate bucked his own party but many pastors couldn't find such courage.

"This is not a game," Cruz said the next day as he defended his convention speech. "Right and wrong matter."[9]

The Cruz moment was perhaps the most significant booing at a Republican convention since Oregon Governor Mark Hatfield and New York Governor Nelson Rockefeller got booed at Goldwater's 1964 nominating convention for daring to condemn the extremism of the racist John Birch Society. When Rockefeller, who refused to endorse Goldwater, finished his remarks, he exited with triumphal waves as if he didn't even hear the booing. The next morning, he proclaimed, "I had the time of my life."[10] Sometimes being booed is a badge of honor.

Across the political aisle, many liberal members of the clergy have also lined up for their partisan team. Campolo, who served as a spiritual advisor for Bill Clinton after his sexual scandals in the White House, urged Christians to vote for Hillary. Numerous African-American pastors also endorsed Clinton. In fact, only Republicans Cruz and Marco Rubio appeared to garner more public pastoral endorsements than Clinton during the primary process (with Carson also grabbing many pastoral endorsements).

Interestingly, the public voices of liberal clergy critiquing Clinton remain quite muted—even on topics like her unethical email practices and her support for wars in Iraq, Libya, and elsewhere. The few liberal voices against Clinton include Cornell West (not a pastor but a professor at Union Theological Seminary). Democrats have for years accused conservative Christians of blindly following the Republican Party no matter what and therefore letting party trump principles. There's some truth to that in previous elections (as well as in this one). But the reverse has also been true as many liberal clergy members will line up behind whoever the Democratic Party nominates. In some ways it seems more true now that liberal pastors and Christian leaders are willing to give their side a pass. While the conservative Christian voices against Trump are a minority, there are at least some prominent figures speaking out on principles. On the left, such prophetic moral critiques are missing. Across the theological and political spectrums, we face a serious test of faith.

It's one thing to show up on election day, grab a ballot, say a prayer, and fill in the box next to Donald J. Trump or Hillary Clinton or someone else. It's quite another to publicly endorse a candidate. When you publicly endorse a candidate, you endorse the policies they advocate and the rhetoric they employ. By publicly endorsing a candidate, pastors will tie their own credibility—and thus the credibility and witness of their churches—to what that candidate says or does. I'm not saying we can't be political (in fact, I'll argue the opposite of that in chapter five). But we must tread carefully.

The 2016 election particularly poses dangers as both major candidates come with serious moral concerns (as will be explored in the next chapter). Even if you think one of them is great, it's important to recognize we have the two least popular nominees in polling history. Trump is the least popular and Clinton is second. More than half of Americans don't like Clinton and about two-thirds don't like Trump. Harry Enten of FiveThirtyEight.com, a site known for its analysis of poll numbers and accurate predictions, explained the "distaste for both Trump and Clinton is record-breaking."[11] Looking at the "net strong favorability ratings" (which takes the number of people who strongly like a candidate and subtracts the number of people who strongly dislike a candidate), he found that Clinton's score is twice as bad the previously most unfavorable candidate—but Trump's score is twice as bad as Clinton's!

"No major party nominee before Clinton or Trump had a double-digit net negative 'strong favorability' rating," he explained. "Clinton's would be the lowest ever, except for Trump."[12]

These numbers should make pastors and Christians stop and think very carefully about offering a public endorsement. Either candidate we choose is disliked by most Americans, and many Americans dislike them both. Do we really want to tie ourselves to sunken ships? To marry one's moral authority and reputation in such a manner is to accept an unequal yoking. It risks the credibility of our churches and ultimately of the gospel message we proclaim. And it risks driving many people away from our churches. We need the prophetic imagination to challenge the system from the margins and offer an alternative approach. It's not about winning; it's about faithfulness.

Savior on Capitol Hill?

Conservative *Washington Post* columnist Michael Gerson, a former chief speechwriter for President George W. Bush, stands out as a prominent voice in 2016 who refuses to let party trump principles. He argued this year's race isn't a normal election when people in the general election go "for pragmatism, give-and-take, holding your nose and eventually getting past an unpleasant chore."[13] Instead, he suggests this campaign is a unique moment where Republican politicians will be remembered by how they stood on Trump. He doesn't support Clinton, but focuses his critique on his fellow Republicans since that's who he thinks he can best impact, that's the party he's most concerned about in the future, and that's the party that's moved the most outside the mainstream with their nominee.

"[I]t is not a normal political moment," Gerson explained. "It is one of those rare times—like the repudiation of Joe McCarthy, or consideration of the Civil Rights Act of 1964, or the Watergate crisis—when the spotlight of history stops on a single decision, and a whole political career is remembered in a single pose. The test here: Can you support, for pragmatic reasons, a presidential candidate who purposely and consistently appeals to racism?"[14]

Even more so, pastors and other Christian leaders will be remembered by where they stood for such a time as this. Did they go all in at the casino mogul's table and walk away with little more than their shirts? Or did they refuse to enter in and therefore kept their moral credibility intact? Come November, the campaign will be over and one of the two candidates will head home. But for pastors and others who offer public endorsements during this campaign, the loss of credibility will last for years. One election—no matter how important—simply isn't worth it. Some are already claiming this is "the most important election of our lives" (as they also claimed in 2012, 2008, 2004…). But even if true, no single U.S. presidential election rivals the importance of our calling from God.

VOTE YOUR CONSCIENCE

Perhaps one lesson we American Christians need to learn in this campaign—and in other parts of our lives—is patience to trust in divine timing. The Hebrew people cried out during slavery in Egypt for more than 400 years before God brought freedom. Later, they wandered in the wilderness for 40 years. A few hundred years later, God's people remained in Babylonian exile for 70 years, and then still had to wait more than 500 years under various oppressive occupations before the birth of the Messiah. Since then, we have been waiting nearly 2,000 years for the return of our King. But we still act like an election for a four-year term is so important that we must do whatever it takes to beat the other side?

In the age of Twitter and texting and Snapchat, four years drag on like an eternity. Yet, when we accept that understanding of time, we've done the opposite of what Paul urged in Romans 12. We've conformed to the world. No longer transformed, we've impatiently joined the world's games and played by the world's rules and quicksand timer. Surely we can endure four-to-eight years without selling our birthright to a charlatan. Even worse, we cave while lavishly living in freedom and wealth. Despite the overheated political rhetoric to the contrary, we're nowhere close to the conditions of Egyptian slavery or Babylonian exile. And we're the ones who are impatient?

Perhaps we need to take a collective deep breath (you know, like for a generation or two). And perhaps we need to avoid the temptation of longing for some supposedly "great" past, which really is more myth than reality.

"Do not say, 'Why is it that the former days were better than these?'" the wise teacher warned us in Ecclesiastes. "For it is not from wisdom that you ask about this."[15]

Discontentment can be dangerous. We lose track of our priorities and our principles. We long for something else, and we're willing to sell out for anyone who promises to give it to us. Even the ancient Hebrew people in the wilderness between Egyptian slavery and the 'promised land' started longing for those supposed 'good ol' days.' They wanted to go back to slavery because they weren't patient to hold to their principles and keep marching forward in faith. What we need today is more prophetic distance from partisan politics. We must engage politicians, but not by hopping in bed with them. We need to be a witness to those in both major parties (and in other parties), not a wing or interest group in just one party. We should offer an alternative message, not just parrot one side's propaganda. We should shine our light, knowing that it will eventually overcome (or trump) the darkness. It might make us seem a bit odd, but that's okay. Charles Marsh, a professor of religion at the University of Virginia, noted "[t]he partisan captivity of the gospel in the United States" has led to us losing our status as a "peculiar people."[16]

"It is time for Christians in the United States to live again like strangers in a strange land," he added. "This does not require our withdrawal from the world or disengagement from politics and culture. It means that we learn to act and to think, to read and to interpret, to organize and to vote, out of the new light springing from the gospel."[17]

I offer this book as a call to a different path, a different kind of politics. Thus, this book is really less about Trump or Clinton and more about our calling as Christians. We'll start in chapter two by considering moral issues at stake in this presidential election. Chapter three considers the issue of identity politics and the role religion has played so far in the 2016 campaign. Chapter four looks at how we got to the current state of religion and politics in the U.S., including how we came to the point of closely aligning our faith with partisan politics. Chapter five explores important religious concepts that carry strong political implications. That chapter considers the inherent political nature of our faith, and therefore why we must be careful not to pollute that politics with a competing kingdom's work. Chapter six offers a call for the church to reignite its prophetic imagination and offer alternative messages in this polarizing presidential campaign. Following that, the appendices (which I believe really are needed), are some related short essays I've published elsewhere. Each essay offers ways to reconsider this current campaign and its rhetoric. My prayer is this book will add to thoughtful Christian dialogue about religion and politics in 2016 and help the church be the church even in the midst of a nasty political campaign.

We are not the saviors of the world. And our would-be leaders in Washington, D.C., are definitely not. Musician Derek Webb captured it well it in his song "A Savior on Capitol Hill" on his brilliant album *Mockingbird*:

You can always trust the devil or a politician

To be the devil or a politician

... We'll never have a savior on Capitol Hill

Later in the song, Webb prophetically mocks the mindset of those who think electing the right president will save our nation:

All of our problems gonna disappear

When we can whisper right in that President's ear

VOTE YOUR CONSCIENCE

He could walk right across the reflection pool

In his combat boots and ten-thousand-dollar suit

You can render unto Caesar, everything that's his

You can trust in his power to come to your defense

It's the way of the world, the way of the gun

It's the trading of an evil for a lesser one

Regardless who wins, we are to remain faithful. Perhaps a silver lining of the 2016 campaign is it seems destined to help us sort out Christian leaders to determine who are really partisans first as they put their party ahead of their principles. The siren call of power is hard to resist. May we keep steering away so the church can be the church. May each of us find the courage to vote our conscience.

"Light Trumps Darkness." Amen!

A church sign I saw one night in July of 2016.

VOTE YOUR CONSCIENCE

Chapter 2: A Moral Dilemma

In our two-party political system, opposing (or even merely critiquing) one candidate often gets misread as inherently supporting the other. In countries with multiple major parties, critiques such as this book can be issued with less of such a problem. If there are five major candidates, opposing one doesn't necessarily mean one must also endorse one of the four alternatives. So whenever someone criticizes Donald Trump, his defenders quickly claim that person just wants President Hillary Clinton (and vice versa whenever someone criticizes Clinton). So let me be clear: I do not plan on voting for Clinton. I have never supported her. Of the three major Democratic candidates (along with Senator Bernie Sanders and former Governor Martin O'Malley), I always viewed her as the most problematic. I was glad she lost the 2008 nomination and hoped history would repeat itself this time.

As noted in the previous chapter, 2016 gives us the two least popular nominees in polling history. They've earned that status. Trump sits far outside the mainstream of modern U.S. politics, lacking the experience, knowledge, temperament, or morals to serve (as we'll explore in this chapter). Historically unpopular, this election shouldn't even be close. The only reason it is close is the Democratic Party nominated Clinton, who brings her own baggage of ethical scandals. Had the Republicans not nominated Trump, Clinton would be the least popular nominee ever and likely lose. Trump and Clinton both only have a chance because of each other.

I have some serious concerns about Clinton, which I'll quickly address. But I'll first note one smaller concern. I remain worried about our nation giving too much power to too few families. We have more than 300 million Americans and yet we seem stuck with a couple of families in the White House. That's not healthy. We don't need another President Clinton just like we don't need another another President Bush. So I was glad Jeb! flamed out this year, just as I was glad Hillary lost the nomination in 2008. I hope we soon elect a female president—just like I'm glad we finally dented the racial barrier to the Oval Office. But I wish that first Madam President would emerge as someone who hadn't already lived in the White House for eight years. Despite that, it will still be a significant moment for our nation if we elect a female president this year. But there are much greater moral concerns about Clinton.

Unethical Governance

Clinton has been in the national spotlight for a quarter-of-a-century, and one thing keeps swirling back: ethical scandals. While

Republicans have blown some issues out of proportion (as Democrats have against some Republican politicians), there are numerous ethical lapses that should worry us about Clinton. Additionally, the fact that she keeps getting caught taking ethical shortcuts or trying to unethically hide information from the public shows a serious character flaw. We're not talking about a one-time mistake or some supposed "right-wing conspiracy." What we see is a pattern of abuse. I'm not going to relitigate the scandals of the 1990s. We should remember, however, that just because she hasn't been charged with legal violations doesn't mean she's been ethical. Those are different standards.

In her most recent—and most important—governmental position as Secretary of State, Clinton showed an inability or unwillingness to follow the rules. In doing so, she put national security at risk and placed herself above the rules expected of everyone else. Most notably, her email and server practices remain highly problematic—especially as she lies about her misdeeds, refuses to repent, and apparently hasn't learned from her mistakes. She used a personal email for business purposes, which she wasn't authorized to do. She housed her own servers in her unsecured basement, which she wasn't authorized to do. She used personal devices (like a Blackberry) for such information, which she wasn't authorized to do. She destroyed thousands of business emails, which she wasn't authorized to do. And she repeatedly lied to the public about all of these matters. Clinton and her campaign falsely say others—like Colin Powell—did the same things. But Powell only made some of the mistakes she did and he did so before some rule changes. Yet, even if true, that's a lousy justification. It's like a criminal arguing a judge shouldn't offer a prison sentence because some other people got away with the same thing. Powell isn't running for president. Clinton broke the rules. Leaders should be held to a higher standard (especially those wanting a promotion).

Independent fact-checkers—who are harsher overall on Trump than Clinton—have been clear she's not telling the facts about her email and servers, including FactCheck.org[1] and Poltifact.com.[2] More damaging to Clinton's credibility, two governmental reports this year blasted her actions. The U.S. Department of State's Office of Inspector General released a report in May of 2016 that documented how Clinton's email and server practices deviated from official rules and common practices.[3] Two months later, the FBI concluded its investigation. Although the FBI recommended against filing charges due to the difficulty of proving malicious intent and the narrow scope of governing statues, FBI Director James Comey issued a brutal critique of Clinton's email and server practices. Lack of charges doesn't absolve Clinton, as Comey made clear. Comey noted Clinton didn't fully remove State Department emails and information from decommissioned servers, sent and received emails with information classified at the time of sending, and failed to turn over thousands of work-related emails. Comey called Clinton and her colleagues "extremely careless in their handling of very sensitive, highly classified information."[4] Two days later, Comey addressed the issue further in a U.S. House Committee on Oversight and Governmental Reform hearing. He again noted Clinton's email and server practices were "unauthorized" and that she made untrue public statements defending her actions.[5] He also stressed that just because there weren't charges that doesn't mean there wouldn't be "consequences" for an active governmental official who acted similarly. More investigations remain, including if she lied under oath to Congress.

These facts are clear: Clinton violated rules and common practices for email and server use in several ways. Then she lied repeatedly to the public—and still hasn't come fully clean as her campaign continues to spin the findings from the governmental reports. And she hasn't fully apologized, which should make us assume she's not learned her lesson and may try some similar scheme once back in office. This unethical governance and public deception must not be excused or dismissed. The prophets in the Old Testament focused much of their critiques on rulers. We, too, should demand a higher standard for those serving in and seeking high office. Unethical actions by our nation's leaders trickle down into our society. If a secretary of state or a president can get away with bending the rules, that teaches others—especially younger Americans whose ethical standards and worldviews are still being molded—to also consider stepping over moral lines. We must demand better from our would-be leaders.

Politicians across the political spectrum—from Senator Bernie Sanders to President Barack Obama to Republican John McCain—have worked to reduce the ability of the wealthy to essentially buy elections and rig the system to favor themselves over the poor (which is a problem the Old Testament prophets spent a lot of time condemning). Like Trump, Clinton represents a step backward in tackling the over-influence of wealth on our politics. In the New Testament, Paul perhaps spells out why a ruler's quest for money proves so dangerous. He famously warned us that "the love of money is a root of all kinds of evil."[6] We see that truth in the kings of ancient Israel who stole land and wealth while the people suffered. We see that truth in various modern settings as corrupt rulers steal from the public coffers to live in decedent palaces while their people starve. And yet, we've nominated two people who've shown a willingness to bend the rules in pursuit of money.

"Like a roaring lion or a charging bear is a wicked ruler over a helpless people,"[7] we find in Proverbs. "By justice a king gives a country stability, but those who are greedy for bribes tear it down."[8]

The Clinton Foundation raises numerous troubling questions about mixing money and power. Several cases exist of foreign donors giving large sums of money to the Clinton Foundation while those same foreign donors found their interests helped along by Secretary Clinton approving a request or removing a hurdle. For instance, when the Russian atomic energy agency sought to take over a large stake of the global uranium business, Clinton had to sign off on the deal as Secretary of State since the U.S. considers uranium a national security issue.[9] As the Russians took over the uranium market, contributions of more than $8 million poured into the Clinton Foundation from key leaders involved in the deal. Adding to the problems, the Clintons didn't publicly identify these donations, but the donations were discovered from other sources.

Many of donations to the Foundation during Clinton's time as Secretary of State raise questions about arms deals. Clinton's State

Department authorized $151 billion of arms deals to 16 nations who donated to the Clinton Foundation (with total donations received somewhere between $54 and $141 million).[10] That amounted to a 143 percent increase in arms sales to those nations when compared to the same time in the George W. Bush administration. Overall arms sales approved only increased 80 percent, so donating nations fared much better than average. Among the donating nations who received approval for arms deals were authoritarian regimes with poor human rights records—like Algeria, Kuwait, Oman, Qatar, Saudi Arabia, and United Arab Emirates. U.S. arms makers selling those weapons also contributed several million dollars to the Clinton Foundation while Secretary Clinton approved $163 billion in contracts for them. Beyond arms sales, there are numerous other settings where it appears there was a collusion between money and power, such as in Colombia, Haiti, and Rwanda. In addition to the donations to the Foundation, Bill Clinton made lots of money in speaking fees from individuals, businesses, and nations benefiting from State Department approval of deals.

Even if there's no smoking gun to prove a *quid pro quo*, these and other deals don't stand above the appearance of wrongdoing. Clinton actually promised during her Senate confirmation hearings for Secretary of State that she and the Foundation would "protect against even the appearance of a conflict of interest."[11] That hasn't happened. Instead, her family and her family's Foundation raked in tons of money as she cut deals with foreign donors. These international deals and decisions will continue with Clinton as president (and will be more serious than when she was merely Secretary of State). We must demand better from our would-be leaders.

Rejection of the Sanctity of Life

Few politicians—and regrettably, few Christians—adhere to a consistent life ethic. The label "pro-life" is generally used only to mean one is anti-abortion. While that's an important life issue, if one's only concerned about life for the 10 months prior to birth that hardly makes one pro-life. Some faith traditions—like Catholics and Mennonites—do a better job than most in advocating for a broader understanding of life. In the early 1980s, Catholic Cardinal Joseph Bernardin in Chicago popularized the idea of a "consistent ethic of life," which is sometimes also known as a "seamless garment of life" (a play on the seamless robe Jesus wore before his crucifixion). This approach urges opposition to abortion, capital punishment, assisted suicide, euthanasia, nuclear weapons, and most (if not all) war. This philosophy also includes concerns for healthcare access, poverty reduction, and environmental care. So when I use the label "pro-life," I mean this broader concept of life. Someone who is merely opposed to abortion I instead call "anti-abortion."

"Many are not accustomed to thinking about all the life-threatening and life-diminishing issues with such consistency," Bernardin explained. "The result is that they remain somewhat selective in their response."[12]

"Precisely because life is sacred, the taking of even one life is a momentous event," he added. "The theological assertion that the human person is made in the image and likeness of God, the philosophical affirmation of the dignity of the person, and the political principle that society and state exist to serve the person—all these themes stand behind the consistent ethic."[13]

A prophetic voice in U.S. society, Bernardin confounded politicians and transcended partisan labels with his moral critiques. He offered a prophetic challenge to both major parties for failing to seek a consistent ethic of life. We need his voice today as we face perhaps the two least pro-life nominees in modern U.S. politics. Trump now espouses an anti-abortion position (which he calls "pro-life"), but it's a recent conversion and his flip-flops on other policies should make us skeptical. While Clinton represents a more pro-life position than Trump in a couple of areas, she generally offers a dreadful life ethic.

Clinton remains strongly pro-choice, only supporting limited restrictions on very late-term abortions. When Bill Clinton ran for office, he argued abortion should be "safe, legal, and rare." Hillary Clinton used to echo that language, such as when she ran in 2008. But in 2016, Clinton instead pledges to protect "safe, legal abortion."[14] That's a profound difference as the former position at least attempts to fight causes of unwanted pregnancies and even suggests abortion shouldn't be common. She also pushes for a repeal of the ban on using taxpayer funding for abortion, which means those who oppose abortion wouldn't have the choice to not fund it. There are some Democrats who favor more restrictions on abortions, like West Virginia Senator Joe Manchin and Louisiana Governor John Bel Edwards. The anti-abortion group Democrats for Life notes that one-third of Democrats fall in that camp. Clinton's running mate, Senator Tim Kaine of Virginia, is a devout Catholic who views abortion as wrong even though his voting record is quite pro-choice. Yet, in four years as governor of Virginia, he likely did more to reduce actual abortions than Trump's done in his whole life. Even if one disagrees with Kaine's voting record, his comments about abortion show something quite different from Clinton's rhetoric.

On another life issue, a significant shift occurred this year in the Democratic platform. For the first time, the party took a stand for abolishing the death penalty. This, however, stands in opposition to Clinton's opinion. The platform change is the result of Senator Bernie Sanders and his allies working to move the party on key issues. Clinton still supports capital punishment despite the fact that it doesn't serve as a deterrent to crime, innocent individuals have been executed and hundreds of others were convicted and imprisoned before exoneration, and a clear racial disparity that makes it more likely for racial minorities to receive capital punishment. With Sanders and his allies successfully changing the party platform, Clinton sits outside her own party's embrace of a better life ethic. Her running mate, Kaine, opposes the death penalty. In fact, before he ran for public office he even served as a pro-bono attorney for individuals on death row. If you're interested in learning more about why we as Christians should oppose the death penalty, read Shane Claiborne's new book *Executing Grace: How the Death Penalty Killed Jesus and Why It's Killing Us*.[15]

A final—and significant—area of life where Clinton remains highly problematic comes with her hawkish foreign policy. She would not only embrace a much more militaristic and violent foreign policy than President Barack Obama, but would move the nation closer to starting more wars. She supported the invasion of Iraq in 2003, which destabilized the region and helped spark the rise of ISIS. Trump also offered his support for that war back then. The impact of that preemptive war based on lies about weapons of mass destruction led to the near-extinction of the historic Christian community in Iraq. Prior to the U.S. invasion, nearly 1.5 million Christians lived in Iraq (or more than 6 percent of the population). Today, Christians in the war-torn nation are estimated to total less than 300,000. That means 80 percent of the Christian community in Iraq, which dates back to the first century, has either been killed or forced to flee to other nations. More than 150,000 Iraqi civilians have likely been killed in violence since the U.S. invasion.

Unfortunately, Iraq does not represent a one-time error of judgment for Clinton. As a senator, she bucked most Democrats in backing continued sales of cluster bombs to other nations. Since it's an explosive that often kills and maims civilians, more than 100 nations have signed an international treaty banning them. The U.S. has not. Clinton played a key leadership role in the military action in Libya in 2011. While Vice President Biden and other top administration officials pressed against military involvement, Clinton made the case for intervening.[16] Although not as horrific as the Iraq invasion, the war still further destabilized Libya and resulted in many civilian deaths and some American deaths. As Secretary of State, Clinton also pushed for the U.S. to help funnel weapons into Syria to add to that nation's bloody and chaotic civil war.[17] In her 2016 campaign, she's also pushed for more U.S. military involvement in that war. One week before Clinton officially received her party's nomination, U.S. airstrikes in Syria mistakenly targeted a group of civilians. Between 70 and 130 civilians were killed in that one strike. U.S. media largely buried the story just days after banner attention to a terrorist attack in Nice, France, that killed 84 civilians. Our strikes have killed hundreds of more Syrian civilians during the conflict. As Christians, we must lament the loss of any civilian lives, not just Western ones. And if our government is responsible for the terror, we have an extra burden to speak out.

Due to the release of Clinton's emails, we better understand her foreign policy philosophy, which sadly seems to follow the old Cold War strategy of promoting coups against democratically-elected leaders we don't like. When a military coup erupted in Honduras in 2009, world leaders strongly condemned it as illegal and illegitimate. However, Secretary Clinton instead quickly reached out to the coup leaders to offer support and recognition.[18] The homicide rate in

Honduras spiked in the years following the coup, sending droves of migrant children fleeing northward to the United States. Clinton then claimed those kids should be sent back to the violent nation she helped destabilize. Where did Clinton get such foreign policy ideas? Perhaps from her friend Henry Kissinger, who wrecked nations across the globe during his time in U.S. leadership. She doesn't just count him as an expert to consult, but has even vacationed with him in the Dominican Republic. Kissinger prolonged the Vietnam War, led the U.S. to illegally bomb Laos and Cambodia, plotted assassinations of political leaders in various nations we weren't even at war with, and contributed to destabilization and numerous deaths in countries like Afghanistan, Bangladesh, and East Timor.

Clinton runs on her foreign policy experience. She does bring a lot of experience to the table, but it's a record of backing disastrous wars and military interventions. We don't know what Trump would do; he might spark irrational wars simply because someone criticized him on Twitter, but he also shows an isolationist streak that could lead to fewer military actions. But Clinton's record remains clear: she'll back more aggressive military actions. I fear as president she will continue to throw ammo on fiery conflicts around the world, creating more instability and higher body counts. We're not playing a game of 'Risk.' This is real life where real people die.

A Moral Case Against Donald Trump

I'll offer five overall areas on why Christians shouldn't support Donald Trump: his vulgar misogyny, his religious bigotry, his promotion of violence, his authoritarian tendencies, and his racism.

Vulgar Misogyny

Words matter. Words tell us a lot about the person uttering them. It's the advice we find in the book written by James (a brother of Jesus and an early church leader).

"The tongue also is a fire, a world of evil among the parts of the body," James warned us. "It corrupts the whole body, sets the whole course of one's life on fire, and is itself set on fire by hell."[19]

"With the tongue we praise our Lord and Father, and with it we curse human beings, who have been made in God's likeness," he added. "Out of the same mouth come praise and cursing. My brothers and sisters, this should not be. Can both fresh water and salt water flow from the same spring? My brothers and sisters, can a fig tree bear olives, or a grapevine bear figs? Neither can a salt spring produce fresh water."[20]

So let's consider Trump's words. At campaign rallies, he's used the following words (only without the edits): h**l, son-a-b***h, p***y, b*****d, s**t, bulls**t, f**k, f**king, and mother***ers. And that's just during official campaign speeches! These aren't private profanities secretly recorded; these are words he repeatedly uses as he seeks to lead our nation. Often kids are at campaign rallies. It's not just that they hear such language; they hear such words as the way a presidential nominee talks. While some politicians across the political spectrum—like Republican John McCain and Democrat Joe Biden—occasionally drop an obscenity into a speech, Trump's profanity is something quite different. It's the difference between a 'PG-13' and an 'R' rating for a movie. Perhaps we need an age restriction on Trump campaign rallies! My concern about the degrading of public discourse with f-bombs might make me a bit of a Puritan. But before you decide to back Trump, you need to ask yourself if you're okay with the potty-mouth in the presidential bully pulpit. Is this the role model you want for your children and grandchildren? It's one thing for a reality TV celebrity to talk like that. It's another thing for our nation's leader.

As if the profanity alone didn't raise enough concerns, Trump's vulgar rhetoric also shows his misogyny (prejudice against women) as he trashes women and treats them like nothing more than sexual property. Over twenty years, Trump appeared a couple of dozen times on shock jock Howard Stern's radio show. Much of the banter between Trump and Stern came as Trump bragged about women he'd slept with or women he would like to.[21] As he discussed various celebrities he'd like to sleep with (or not), he critiqued their physical features—especially their boobs—to justify his desires. He talked about oral sex, his sexual practices with his girlfriend (now wife), and whether he could have an erection for a particular woman. These aren't ancient remarks, instead all occurring since 2000. On other occasions, he also offered a low view of women.[22] He's frequently claimed that nearly all the women around him flirt with him and want to sleep with him. He's compared women to nice things to look at, like buildings and art. He described his girlfriend as "a young and beautiful piece of a**." He also reportedly called working mothers who pump breastmilk "disgusting."

Trump pals around with *Playboy*'s Hugh Hefner, including attending parties at the Playboy Mansion and smiling on the cover of the magazine with a playmate. That cover hangs framed on Trump's office wall. The cover went viral after Jerry Falwell, Jr. tweeted an image of him and Trump both smiling and holding a thumb up (with Falwell's wife also standing there in the photo).[23] In the background of the photo is the *Playboy* cover. Guess that's what selling out looks like! It's a far cry from when Jerry Falwell, Sr. and other conservative Christian activists criticized Jimmy Carter for giving an interview with *Playboy*. Carter didn't pose on the cover with a playmate and in the interview he offered a good summary of the 'Sermon on the Mount' about adultery including lusting in one's heart. Yep, Carter basically called out every single reader of the magazine within its very pages! Even then he received criticism for lending credibility to the publication. Trump didn't try to convert anyone, but instead celebrated that lifestyle—and continues to with the framed cover on his office wall even when inviting hundreds of pastors to stop by. Additionally, Trump made an unusual remark about Jesus in that *Playboy* interview. After Trump claimed "[e]very successful person has a very large ego," the interviewer asked, "Every successful person? Mother Teresa? Jesus Christ?"[24] Trump responded, "Far greater egos than you will ever understand."[25] With that remark, Trump showed little understanding of Jesus—who humbled himself to death on a cross (see Philippians 2:5-8)—and Trump instead remade Jesus into his own egotistical image. I'll give that two thumbs down.

During the campaign, Trump continued his misogyny. After the first Republican presidential debate, Trump pushed an attack on Megyn Kelly of *Fox News* as a "bimbo" and suggested she was hormonal during the debate as he said Kelly "had blood coming out of her eyes, blood coming out of her wherever."[26] He attacked her for noting his history of misogyny. A month later, he attacked Republican presidential hopeful Carly Fiorina not on issues but looks: "Look at that face! Would anyone vote for that? Can you imagine that, the face of our next president?"[27] Later he even attacked the appearance of the wife of his opponent Ted Cruz. On another occasion in the campaign, he used a Yiddish word for a man's genitals to describe how Hillary Clinton had lost to Barack Obama in 2008. Trump's even attacked Hillary for Bill Clinton's affairs (suggesting she's to blame), which is particularly ironic coming from a serial philander like Trump!

While Trump flip-flops on many issues, his misogyny appears quite consistent. It's a core part of who he is. We can't say we're somehow endorsing him, but not endorsing his words. His vulgar words are a window to his heart. In fact, he's made it a key image to brag about, essentially arguing he must be a great and smart man winning at life because of the all the women who sleep with him. Women are objects for him to look at and use to stroke his own ego—

and this has even included his own daughter as he described her body and said he'd date her if she wasn't his daughter. Since the Republican convention, he's even defended a sexual harasser and suggested it's the fault of women if they're harassed. If we take seriously the words of Paul—"nor is there male and female, for you are all one in Christ Jesus"[28]—we can't condone the sexism and vulgarity of Trump. Conservative Christians used to preach against this type of boorish behavior. His talk isn't right in the locker room, let alone the public square. This isn't a matter of 'political correctness.' This is about decency and respect for women. Popular Christian author and pastor Max Lucado put it well.

"Such insensitivities wouldn't be acceptable even for a middle school student body election," he wrote in a viral post. "But for the Oval Office? And to do so while brandishing a Bible and boasting of his Christian faith?" [29]

"I'm a pastor," he added. "I don't endorse candidates or place bumper stickers on my car. But I am protective of the Christian faith. If a public personality calls on Christ one day and calls someone a 'bimbo' the next, is something not awry? And to do so, not once, but repeatedly, unrepentantly and unapologetically? We stand against bullying in schools. Shouldn't we do the same in presidential politics?"[30]

VOTE YOUR CONSCIENCE

Words matter. And what words we associate with matter.

Religious Bigotry

As a Baptist minister, I'm proud of the Baptist heritage of fighting for religious liberty for all. Thomas Helwys, one of the first two Baptist leaders, in 1612 wrote the first call in English for religious liberty for all people (as opposed to the usual argument of people just demanding freedoms for their own people). Early Baptists in the U.S. like Roger Williams and Isaac Backus preached this message of religious liberty for all. Thomas Jefferson's usage of the phrase "wall of separation between church and state" came in a letter to Baptists in Connecticut because he knew the Baptists would appreciate that philosophy. Were it not for the tireless advocacy of Baptist preacher John Leland, the religious freedoms in the First Amendment to the U.S. Constitution might not exist. It turns out that separation of church and state is good for both (especially the ice cream). Brent Walker, executive director of the Baptist Joint Committee for Religious Liberty (which unites 15 Baptist bodies in the U.S. to advocate and educate for religious liberty), explained the key issue well during testimony to the U.S. Senate Judiciary Committee.

"The best thing government can do for religion is to leave it alone," he explained. "[T]he painful lessons of history teach that when government takes sides in religion—for or against—someone's religious liberty is denied and everyone's is threatened."[31]

Walker's right. And, unfortunately, we've seen various faith traditions come under fire at different points in our political history. Mitt Romney faced criticism in 2012 for being Mormon. Barack Obama faced criticism in 2008 over false accusations he's a Muslim. Jimmy Carter faced criticism in 1976 for being 'born again.' John F. Kennedy faced criticism in 1960 for being Catholic. And I could keep going back in time. When we condone faith-based attacks against others in one election, we set the precedents that could put our own faith in the crosshairs during the next campaign.

Religious liberty remains an important issue. In fact, religious liberty is quickly becoming a key phrase used by conservative Christians to justify supporting Trump. But if religious liberty is something you care about—and I think it should be—then you must reject Trump. When the topic of religious liberty came up during the February 25, 2016 Republican debate, Trump demonstrated a lack of any understanding of the depth of this critical First Amendment issue. Rather than answer the question, he repeatedly changed the subject. This shouldn't surprise us since Trump demonstrated throughout the campaign that he doesn't believe in religious liberty. After all, he consistently attacked people based on their religion.

Trump first questioned Ben Carson's faith and conversion. Regardless what one may think of Carson politically, his faith credentials were well-established long before he ran for president. After Carson briefly took the lead in the polls in Iowa, Trump argued Carson lied about his conversion experience.

"How stupid are the people of Iowa?" Trump ranted as he recounted Carson's conversion story. "How stupid are the people of this country to believe this crap?"[32]

"What he's saying is that these series of events and he goes into the bathroom for a couple of hours and he comes out, and now he's religious and the people of Iowa believe him," Trump added. "Give me a break. Give me a break. It doesn't happen that way. It doesn't happen that way. ... Don't be fools."[33]

Trump's rhetoric should concern evangelicals who believe that is actually how someone could come to faith. As if all of that wasn't bad enough, Trump also attacked Carson's church, the Seventh-Day Adventists. The denomination has historically faced suspicions and accusations of being cult-like, so Trump used a conspiratorial tone to try and score political points by attacking a church.

"I'm Presbyterian," Trump said at a campaign rally. "Boy, that's down the middle of the road folks, in all fairness. I mean, Seventh-day Adventist, I don't know about. I just don't know about."[34]

When asked to apologize, he refused and continued to conspiratorially suggest there were things we don't know about that denomination (though a quick visit to Wikipedia could've solved that). If we're hiring a pastor or religious leader, we can debate theological differences between Seventh-day Adventists and Presbyterians and Baptists. But for a political office, a candidate's faith doesn't matter. Lying and hypocrisy can be legitimate voting concerns, but not someone's religious affiliation. Whisper campaigns like those Trump used against the Seventh-day Adventists must be rejected by anyone who cares about religious liberty. It may be Seventh-day Adventists today, but tomorrow it'll be someone else. Like Southern Baptists and Methodists.

Trump also used faith-based attacks on Senator Ted Cruz, a Southern Baptist. Cruz's dad immigrated to the U.S. from Cuba, later experiencing a 'born-again' conversion and becoming a pastor. Ted Cruz got saved and baptized as a child at Clay Road Baptist Church in

Houston, graduated from Second Baptist High School in Houston, and is a member at First Baptist Church in Houston. Yet, Trump—who would later bizarrely claim Cruz's dad was somehow involved in the assassination of John F. Kennedy—used conspiratorial logic to attack the faith of Cruz as the two battled for evangelical voters in Iowa.

"To the best of my knowledge, not too many evangelicals come out of Cuba, okay?" Trump said as a rally. "Just remember that. Just remember."[35]

"In all fairness, here we are," Trump added as he held up a Bible as a political prop. "Just remember that, folks. When you're casting your ballot, remember. I have a lot of support, lot of support from amazing people. Franklin Graham said incredible things about me the other day. We have so many pastors and so many ministers in favor, and it's just very important to me."[36]

Trump repeated the claim that not many evangelicals come from Cuba in numerous speeches. It's odd for several reasons. Cruz didn't come from Cuba, Cruz' dad converted in the U.S., and it's just factually wrong. I've been to Cuba twice and have met many Baptist pastors there. There are evangelicals doing amazing ministry in Cuba and their churches are growing. They probably have a few things to teach us evangelicals in the U.S. about church planting! You can find a bit more about my thoughts on Baptists in Cuba in appendix five. This attempt to define one's faith by nationality goes against basic Christian teachings. You aren't saved based on your heritage or place of birth!

Already Trump's brought his religious-based attacks into the general election by attacking Hillary Clinton's faith. Regardless of what one thinks of her politically—and, as I've noted, there are serious reasons to not vote for her—her faith should be out-of-bounds. And if we're going to consider her faith, it's clear that like Carson and Cruz she's much more devout than Trump.

"We don't know anything about Hillary in terms of religion," Trump claimed in a meeting with conservative pastors. "Now, she's been in the public eye for years and years, and yet there's no—there's nothing out there."[37]

Like his conspiratorial attack on Carson where Trump suggested he just didn't know, his attack on Clinton's faith is inaccurate and inappropriate. If we value religious liberty, we'll judge the candidates on their merits and reject anyone—like Trump—who suggests we should make faith-based voting assessments. If Trump truly believed in religious liberty, he would steer clear of these types of attacks on Carson, Cruz, Clinton, and others. Instead he turned out to be the worst offender—by a huge margin—during the 2016 campaign.

As if his attacks on the faith of his electoral opponents weren't bad enough (and they are), Trump's biggest offense in the area of religious liberty came in his policy proposals regarding Muslims. Perhaps Trump's second most famous policy proposal during the campaign (and we'll deal with the top one soon) came as he suggested banning any Muslim from entering the United States. It wasn't some off-the-cuff idea; this came in an official press release and he stood by it on numerous occasions. He also argued for surveillance of mosques, perhaps even closing down mosques, creating a federal database of Muslims living the U.S., and perhaps giving Muslims a special I.D. (but no word yet if he wants them to wear a special armband). This is nothing short of religious bigotry and the creation of a religious test to treat certain people as second-class citizens (or less). Trump's also attacked Muslims in other ways, often with false, conspiratorial claims. A report by Georgetown University's Center for Muslim-Christian Understanding noted the presidential rhetoric by Trump has sparked a rise in physical violence against U.S. Muslims, (including incidents where Trump supporters chanted "Trump" as they attacked Muslims) and a rise in attacks on mosques.[38]

Russell Moore of the Southern Baptist Convention's Ethics & Religious Liberty Commission, offered a forceful critique of Trump's

Muslim ban proposal. Moore even defends the right of Muslims to worship freely at their mosques—because to do otherwise is to reject the principle of religious liberty.

"It is not in spite of our gospel conviction, but precisely because of it, that we should stand for religious liberty for everyone," Moore argued. "Make no mistake. A government that can shut down mosques simply because they are mosques can shut down Bible studies because they are Bible studies. A government that can close the borders to all Muslims simply on the basis of their religious belief can do the same thing for evangelical Christians. A government that issues ID badges for Muslims simply because they are Muslims can, in the fullness of time, demand the same for Christians because we are Christians."[39]

When we create the precedent of imposing religious tests and religious persecution on one group, it empowers the government to take similar actions against others. Trump's proposals are truly dangerous. If we believe in real religious liberty, we must reject demagogues who peddle religious bigotry and seek to codify religious persecution. If someone invokes the principle of religious liberty to justify supporting Trump, they either haven't paid attention to Trump or they don't believe in true religious liberty for all.

VOTE YOUR CONSCIENCE

Promotion of Violence

As Jerry Falwell, Jr. and about 1,000 pastors arrived on Broadway in New York City to meet with Trump in June, one guy stood there greeting them. He knew many of them. But he wasn't smiling. He held a handwritten sign that declared:

Torture is not pro-life

Racism is not pro-life

Misogyny is not pro-life

Murdering the children of terrorists is not pro-life

Proverbs 29:2[40]

The man holding the sign? Eric Teetsel, who ran the faith outreach for Senator Marco Rubio's presidential campaign. Some of those filing past him had endorsed Rubio. Others had worked with Teetsel before the campaign on other conservative religious-political efforts. But while they arrived for political access, he stood outside with a prophetic reminder. It does seem the prophets often stand alone on the narrow path while everyone else heads down the broad way.

"Christians are called to live out the Gospel in every aspect of their lives, including politics," Teetsel said. "It matters. It's important. But we have to be sure that we are representing the Gospel in truth. ... I think we know enough about Donald Trump to know that a Christian response should be prayer for him, but also a prophetic witness about what is true."[41]

Teetsel's right that we need to stand as a prophetic witness to Trump's embrace of a culture of death. Beyond the violence Trump's inspired against Muslims, he's promoted violence in many other ways through his campaign rhetoric and policies. Jesus said, "Blessed are the peacemakers for they will be called children of God."[42] Jesus also said blessed are those who are poor in spirit, mourn, are meek, hunger and thirst for righteousness, are merciful, and are pure in heart—all of which stand in stark contrast to the fruits of Trump! We celebrate Jesus as "the Prince of Peace" and are told to become like him. Each Christmas we celebrate the promise of "peace on Earth." The call to peace isn't merely spiritual peace, but a real-life practical teaching. It's something we can't just preach in church on Sunday; we must also practice peace in the voting booth on Tuesday and how we live each day.

Trump's political rallies quickly gained a reputation as raucous events full of protestors and fights. This isn't a coincidence. There's a reason smoke swirls around a campfire. Throughout his rallies he incited violence, often to the cheers of his crowd as he chuckled and smiled. So we shouldn't be surprised violence occurred. Here are a few examples of Trump inciting violence[43]:

> "He should have been, maybe he should have been roughed up."

> "Knock the crap out of them, would you? Seriously, okay? Just knock the h**l. I promise you I will pay for the legal fees, I promise."

> "Part of the problem and part of the reason it takes so long [to remove protestors] is nobody wants to hurt each other anymore."

> "We're not allowed to punch back anymore. I love the old days. You know what they used to do to guys like that when they were in a place like this? They'd be carried out on a stretcher, folks. ... I'd like to punch him in the face, I'll tell you."

"In the good ol' days this doesn't happen because they used to treat them very, very rough. And when they protested once, you know, they would not do it again so easily."

Where there's smoke, there's fire. And Trump keeps throwing more fuel on it. You won't find remarks like that from other candidates and you won't find the same level of violence in the crowd for other candidates. Making Trump's remarks more problematic, he often made those comments to his nearly all-white crowd as security removed black protestors. What's the approach from 'the good ol' days' he's suggesting should be taken?

Trump's policy proposals also show a love of violence that would be particularly dangerous if given the powers of the presidency. Trump pledged to bring back torture (as sadly several other Republican presidential hopefuls did). Politicians across the political spectrum denounce torture as illegal, unhelpful, and immoral. It's one of the dark stains on President George W. Bush's presidency. President Barack Obama rightly ended the policies that authorized torture and a bipartisan coalition in Congress later voted for a ban to strengthen his executive order. And just in case there's any confusion, waterboarding is torture! It was always described that way throughout history until Bush tried to redefine it in Orwellian doublespeak as an "enhanced interrogation technique." Republican Senator John McCain, who experienced torture as a prisoner of war, said waterboarding is clearly torture and thus remains "prohibited by American laws and values."[44]

"This is a moral debate," he added. "It is about who we are."[45]

Are we willing to become the thing we hate just to win? Are we willing to throw our values away because we're scared? Trump, of course, doesn't respect McCain's comments as Trump even mocked McCain's military service since McCain was a prisoner of war. So Trump embraces waterboarding.

"I would bring back waterboarding and I'd bring back a h**l of a lot worse than waterboarding,"[46] Trump bragged during a Republican debate on February 7.

"They asked me," Trump later recounted about the debate, "'What do you think about waterboarding, Mr. Trump?' I said I love it. I love it, I think it's great. And I said the only thing is, we should make it much tougher than waterboarding."[47]

While other candidates wrongly defended waterboarding, Trump's enthusiastic embrace of an immoral, anti-life practice should stop Christians from supporting him. We worship a tortured King. We don't need a would-be king who praises torture.   In addition to glorifying torture, Trump also proposed a medieval foreign policy of killing innocent women and children. Pledging to "knock the h**l out of" ISIS, he complained we're currently "fighting a very politically correct war."[48] Thus, he proposed a new strategy. His plan for fighting terrorists is to become terrorists ourselves.

"You have to fight fire with fire," Trump claimed. "We have to be so strong. We have to fight so viciously and violently because we're dealing with violent people viciously."[49]

"The other thing with the terrorists is you have to take out their families, when you get these terrorists, you have to take out their families," he also said. "They care about their lives, don't kid yourself. When they say they don't care about their lives, you have to take out their families."[50]

Such a policy not only violates international law, but is also immoral. Trump's idea of becoming fire to put out fire is wrong. What puts out fire is not more fire but something completely different like water or sand. Becoming terrorists to fight terrorists doesn't stop terrorism. It actually increases it because now we are terrorists (and also probably inspires more terrorists in response). Martin Luther King, Jr., a Baptist minister, knew a better approach he learned from the love of Jesus.

"Why should we love our enemies?" King wrote. "Returning hate for hate multiplies hate, adding deeper darkness to a night already devoid of stars. Darkness cannot drive out darkness; only light can do that. Hate cannot drive out hate; only love can do that. Hate multiplies hate, violence multiplies violence, and toughness multiplies toughness in a descending spiral of destruction."[51]

Foreign policy may be the area where a president has the most unchecked power. Economic and other domestic policy proposals generally require congressional support (or can also be undone by the Supreme Court). However, a president can do much (in secrecy and without authorization from Congress) when it comes to military actions. President Obama demonstrates this with his unconstitutional and immoral drone policy where he even has a secret 'kill list' he uses. Imagine giving that power to someone who wants to go even further in killing and in glorifying violence. Imagine allowing someone who praises killing innocent people to have the sole authority to launch a nuclear strike. Trump wants us to believe he's converted to the pro-life cause, but his proposals would allow the killing of small children, pregnant women, and many other innocent people. Eric Teetsel is right: Trump is not pro-life. And to support him as Commander-in-Chief is to back his policies. We can't do that and wear the blessed title of peacemaker.

Authoritarian

During the primaries, some political scientists discovered an interesting social indicator of Trump support. Political scientist and consultant Matthew MacWilliams argued the best predictor of whether someone would support Trump is "authoritarian inclinations."[52]

"Authoritarians obey," MacWilliams explained. "They rally to and follow strong leaders. And they respond aggressively to outsiders, especially when they feel threatened. From pledging to 'make America great again' by building a wall on the border to promising to close mosques and ban Muslims from visiting the United States, Trump is playing directly to authoritarian inclinations."[53]

This doesn't mean all of his supporters are, especially now in the general election. The research caught differences among Republicans in the primary season. Since then we've seen lots of other Republicans who don't like his authoritarian appeals now back him because he's their party's nominee. Looking at his Christian supporters during the primary—which is quite small compared to his Christian supporters since wrapping up the nomination—the authoritarian explanation makes sense. Mark Leary, professor of psychology and neuroscience at Duke University, explained how those holding authoritarian inclinations could attract some Christian leaders since traits include "rigid adherence to traditional values; the tendency to condemn, reject, and punish people who violate those values; and having a submissive, uncritical attitude toward powerful authorities who support and defend one's values and views."[54] Thus, he added, "many of the central messages of the Trump campaign would seem to appeal to such individuals."[55] Compare those traits with the case Robert Jeffress of First Baptist Church of Dallas made for backing Trump early in the primaries.

"I think the same-sex marriage ruling by the Supreme Court last June was a watershed moment for evangelical Christians," he said. "I think in a strange way, that same-sex marriage ruling actually made evangelicals more open to a secular candidate like Donald Trump and here's why. I think many evangelicals have come to the conclusion we can no longer depend upon government to uphold traditional biblical values. Let's just let government solve practical problems like immigration, the economy and national security. And if that's all we're looking for government to do, then we don't need a spiritual giant in the White House. We need a strong leader and a problem solver, hence many Christians are open to a secular candidate like Donald Trump."[56]

In the midst of lamenting the loss of "traditional biblical values," Jeffress longs for a "strong leader" to reject outsiders like immigrants and terrorists. On another occasion while Jeffress defended supporting Trump, Jeffress recounted his answer to being asked if he wanted a candidate who held to what Jesus preached in the 'Sermon on the Mount.'

"Heck no," Jeffress declared. "I would run from that candidate as far as possible, because the Sermon on the Mount was not given as a governing principle for this nation. ... Government is to be a strongman to protect its citizens against evildoers. When I'm looking for somebody who's going to deal with ISIS and exterminate ISIS, I don't care about that candidate's tone or vocabulary, I want the meanest, toughest, son of a you-know-what I can find—and I believe that's biblical."[57]

If we find an election ballot with Jesus versus Trump, Jeffress just announced his endorsement of Trump. Jeffress so longs for an authoritarian strongman that he dismisses the greatest sermon by Jesus as merely pie-in-the-sky rubbish not useful for anything outside of children's Sunday School make-believe. His philosophy's a lot of things, but it's not biblical. This search for a strongman pops up frequently in the pro-Trump remarks of key Christian leaders.

"Evangelicals are wanting a strong leader," Franklin Graham claimed. "They want someone who holds Biblical values, no question … but when it comes to politics, it's hard to find those. I think people are just looking for strong leadership and they see that possibly with Donald Trump."[58]

"Many [evangelicals and conservatives] see Donald Trump as the tough guy who will protect and defend us in perilous times," Falwell similarly declared. "All the other issues will be moot if we don't save the country. … That's why a large majority of them are supporting him, and I think maybe after the country is saved and restored, perhaps evangelicals will start voting in traditional patterns again."[59]

As long as he promises to keep us safe and "make America great," what else could matter? Of the five areas about Trump explored in this chapter, this one's unique. In the other areas, Christian supporters seek to downplay or explain away Trump's sins. They'll say he doesn't really mean it or claim they support him without endorsing those parts of him. But this area—authoritarianism—his Christians supporters actually applaud. They like that he's a strongman. We've seen a version of this story before.

"Give us a king to lead us," the Hebrew people demanded of Judge Samuel. "We want a king over us. Then we will be like all the other nations, with a king to lead us and to go out before us and fight our battles."[60]

Give us a king, a strongman, a fighter, a killer. We want someone other than God as our King. We want someone who will make Israel great again. Samuel warned them what this king would do to them, how the king would take their land and children for his own pleasure and wealth. But they insisted on it anyway. This temptation for a strong ruler continues. Falwell suggested we put aside principles for this election to vote for someone to save our country and then later we can go back to finding principled, godly people. But if the lesson of the ancient Hebrew people is any lesson, once you start down the road of kings, it's hard to overthrow it. Next thing you know, a new king arrives and changes which religion to support.

Trump shows no respect for democratic freedoms, constitutional checks-and-balances, or even rule of law. He's praised strongmen like Russian leader Vladimir Putin, North Korean dictator Kim Jong-un, and former Iraqi dictator Saddam Hussein. That's quite a trio to pick as your wise men to follow. He praises a dictator in Russia who invades countries, takes vindictive actions against journalists and political opponents, and who this year approved new laws to outlaw evangelism by churches and missionaries. He praises a dictator in North Korea who killed his rivals so he could have complete, godlike control over his people. He praises a dictator in Iraq who committed genocide against his own people and supported terrorists in other nations.

Trump's frequently pledged to undo press protections once in office. He's worked to stop reporters from covering his events—trying to keep them trapped in a pen and has ejected any who stray. I received media credentials for a Trump event in Iowa during the primary and snuck out of the press pen without getting caught, so I've seen this ridiculous treatment firsthand that is like nothing I've seen from any other campaign. He even went so far as to ban reporters—and even whole publications like the *Washington Post*—from covering his events once they write a story critical of him. Not even President Richard Nixon, whose downfall came in large part to the reporting of the *Washington Post*, took actions like that against the newspaper. Trump's threatened that once in office he'll investigate the *Post*'s owner and levy additional taxes, and he's promised to end laws that protect the press from frivolous lawsuits (especially by rich celebrities who don't like any coverage that's not glowing). Our nation's founders enshrined the right to a free press in our First Amendment because they saw it as critical to a free society and the necessary check to prevent a demagogue (ahem) from trying to rule like a king. After all, George Washington and others had just fought a revolution to throw off the strongman rule of a king.

Trump's also suggested he'd use the powers of the presidency (and some powers not given to presidents) to go after people who stand in the way of his business interests. This includes a judge he attacked on ethnic grounds who he wants investigated for ruling against him. It also includes the PGA for daring to move a golf tournament from a Trump-owned course (to one in Mexico!), an action he said wouldn't happen if he were president. In various countries we've seen dictators like this as they mix state wealth with their own, stuffing their pockets at the expense of the people.

Trump's attitude on religious liberty shows his strongman tendencies—and I fear that many Christians like that about him. One of his most oft-repeated lines on the campaign trail is complaining about how stores don't say 'Merry Christmas' anymore.

"I always say, we're gonna have a time very soon, when I get elected, when people are going to say 'Merry Christmas' again," Trump told a meeting of pastors in June. "You don't say it right now. You go into the big department stores, they don't have 'Merry Christmas' up. They have 'Happy Holidays,' and now even that is coming under assault. You can't say 'Happy Holidays.' We're becoming so politically correct that we can't function as a country anymore."[61]

I assume no stores had 'Merry Christmas' or 'Happy Holidays' up since it was June! And even in December I don't care since my faith isn't based on what sign Victoria's Secret puts in its window to advertise their half-priced lingerie. Even if you think Trump's right that stores should say that, presidents can't legally force businesses to do that (but strongman dictators can).

"We are going to protect Christianity," Trump claimed while speaking at Liberty University. "And we've got to protect because bad things are happening, very bad things are happening."[62]

We already have a Savior. If someone supports Trump because he'll "protect" Christianity, that's a dangerous concept of the presidency and of Christianity. We don't need a president with the power to pick a faith and force it on individuals and businesses. And we definitely don't need a strongman to help evangelize. Our Savior died at the order of strongman dictators. His love can't be forced on someone with the sword or edict (or business sign). We're playing with fire if we empower a narcissistic, vindictive person with no respect for checks-and-balance or how legal and legislative structures operate.

Racism

Trump launched his recent political popularity with a racist attack on President Barack Obama. As Trump flirted with running for president for the 2012 Republican presidential nomination, he fixated almost entirely on the question of Obama's birth. Trump soon established himself as the celebrity face of the 'birther movement' that falsely claimed Obama's parents somehow snuck him to Kenya to be born and then snuck him back into the U.S. so he could run for president. It's a wild conspiracy theory even for Trump. And this line of attack against the nation's first African-American president shows the ugly underbelly of racism still rampant in our nation. Trump then returned in 2015 to actually run. And he birthed his campaign with a racist attack.

"When Mexico sends its people, they're not sending their best," Trump claimed. "They're not sending you. They're not sending you. They're sending people that have lots of problems, and they're bringing those problems with us. They're bringing drugs. They're bringing crime. They're rapists. And some, I assume, are good people."[63]

"I would build a great wall, and nobody builds walls better than me, believe me, and I'll build them very inexpensively, I will build a great, great wall on our southern border," he added. "And I will have Mexico pay for that wall. Mark my words."[64]

With that, Trump launched his campaign and announced his most well-known policy proposal. And it all started with a racist attack on our southern neighbors. This is the core of the Trump candidacy. One cannot say they back Trump, but not his wall. One cannot say they back Trump, but not his racism. Without the wall and the racism there is no Trump candidacy to back. Early in his campaign, NBC fired Trump for his racist comments. Apparently the 'Peacock' holds stronger moral standards than many Christian pastors! Throughout the campaign, Trump continues to play with racial fires. He refused to denounce the Ku Klux Klan or its former leader David Duke during an interview on CNN. Taking the "I don't know" approach (despite comments in the past showing he did know who Duke is), Trump borrowed a line from the violent, racist, anti-immigrant "American Party" in the mid-1800s. That party is popularly known as the "know nothing party" since members often said they knew nothing when pressed on key issues. Trump similarly borrows the slogan "America First" from anti-Semitic politicians in the 1940s. Trump later said he disavows support from Duke without ever condemning, which Duke and other white nationalists/supremacists saw as a wink in their direction. In fact, white nationalists are particularly excited about Trump's candidacy, bringing fervent support to him at rallies and online. Trump returns the excitement, often retweeting white nationalists and neo-Nazis. In fact, an analysis early in the primary found that more than half of all of the comments Trump retweeted on Twitter were from white nationalists.[65] That doesn't happen by accident.

Trump's also issued false claims blaming African-Americans for violence, pledged to round up and deport 11 million undocumented Latinos (which would include breaking up families by taking parents from their children), attacked Latino journalists based on their ethnicity, encouraged violence against nonviolent African-American protestors, and attacked a judge not on the merits but on the judge's ethnic background. Saying a judge (or anyone else) cannot do their job because of their race or the country where their parents were born is clearly racist. Trump joined other candidates in utilizing anti-refugee, anti-immigrant rhetoric, often using false claims to demonize refugees.

He even bragged he'd look into the eyes of refugee children (who are fleeing genocidal violence) and tell them they can't come into the United States. We worship a Savior who once was one of those Middle Eastern refugee children (as his parents fled to Egypt to avoid genocidal violence). Too often it seems that when Trump says he wants to "Make America Great Again" he actually means "white again."

Ohio Governor John Kasich, one of the 2016 Republican presidential candidates, released an ad that perhaps best sums up the call we all now face. To his credit, Kasich didn't endorse Trump and skipped the Republican convention even though it was held in his own state. Kasich's ad in November of 2015 featured comments from retired Colonel Tom Moe (an Air Force Veteran and P.O.W. during Vietnam). Moe's comments are an updated paraphrase of Martin Niemöller's famous "First they came for the Socialists" poem. Like most German Christians, Niemöller lined up behind Adolf Hitler and his promises to make Germany great again. Unlike most, however, he eventually publicly resisted and spent seven years in concentration camps.

"You might not care if Donald Trump says Muslims must register with their government because you're not one," Moe says in the ad. "And you might not care if Donald Trump says he's going to round up all the Hispanic immigrants, because you're not one. And you might not care if Donald Trump says it's OK to rough up black protesters, because you're not one. And you might not care if Donald Trump wants to suppress journalists, because you're not one. But think about this: if he keeps going and he actually becomes president, he might just get around to you. And you better hope there's someone left to help you."[66]

The issue of racism is one where white Christians like myself should particularly be vigilant, especially those of us coming from traditions that supported slavery and Jim Crow laws and then opposed civil rights and desegregation. Interestingly, a couple of the key white Christian leaders in the 1950s and early 1960s defending segregation and opposing the civil rights movement were Jerry Falwell, Sr. of Liberty University and W. A. Criswell of First Baptist Church of Dallas. Today, another Jerry Falwell and another pastor of First Baptist Church in Dallas (Robert Jeffress) want us to back Trump so he can "make America great again." History may not repeat, but it seems to echo. Randall Balmer, an Episcopalian priest and historian of American religion who teaches at Dartmouth College, documents how the issue that initially mobilized the 'religious right' wasn't abortion (which Criswell and many other evangelicals initially supported), but segregation. In particular, Falwell Sr. and others organized after the

IRS threatened to strip the tax-exempt status of Bob Jones University and other Christian schools that refused to integrate. Thus, Balmer argues that supporting Trump's racism isn't that far off from the original fight.[67]

Talk of returning to the "good ol' days" might sound fine to white Christians who have a mythic image of the 'nice' 1950s. But to African-Americans and other minorities, they know those were godless days where separate meant unequal and they could be killed just for looking at a white person. Because of Trump's blatant racism and bigotry, I understand why many African-American pastors endorse Hillary Clinton (as they probably would've endorsed nearly any Democrat against someone like Trump). Many white Christians backing Trump do so out of a positon of privilege. But African-American pastors recognize the danger Trump poses to their communities and thus oppose him. If white evangelicals back Trump in large numbers, it may set back efforts at racial conciliation among Christians.

We must love our neighbors. We must speak out against those who demonize our neighbors. We must not lend our credibility to support those who attack our neighbors. Racism is not a minor detail about Trump; it's who he is and what he built his campaign on from the beginning. So we must reject Trump's vision of the supposedly-great "again" he wishes to make America. To say we'll overlook Trump's racism and vote for him anyway because of opposition to abortion (even though his track record is shaky) is to deny a truly pro-life position. If we believe in the sanctity of human life, believe that all people are made in the image of God, and believe that Jesus loves and died for all people, then we cannot support or condone the blatant racism Trump preaches. Racism is evil. Not a lesser evil. Just evil.

The Choice

You likely noticed I devoted much more attention to Trump than Clinton. I did so for two reasons. First, more Christian pastors and leaders—especially within my tradition of white evangelical Christians—are publicly lending their support for Trump. He poses the greater temptation we're facing as a community in the 2016 election. Second, Trump sits much further outside the realm of morality. We find ourselves faced with a candidate who poses a unique threat to our politics and our nation. This isn't about party. A Democratic nominee just like Trump—with vulgar, bigoted, violent and racist rhetoric— would deserve similar treatment. And given Trump's past as a Democrat, his previous campaign donations to Hillary Clinton, and his lack of support for many key Republican ideas, he could very easily be a Democrat.

Some Republicans are already making the "vote for the lesser of two evils" argument. That argument is problematic as we must reject both/all forms of evil. But even if one accepts the logic of the "lesser of two evils" argument, that's not a winning point for Republicans this year. The only way one can claim Trump is the lesser evil is if the only test of morality one uses is if there is an 'R' or a 'D' behind a candidate's name. That partisan morality test must firmly be rejected. *Washington Post* columnist Michael Gerson brings impressive conservative Republican credentials to his "never Trump" arguments he's maintained even after Trump garnered the nomination. Gerson served as President George W. Bush's chief speechwriter from 2001 to 2006. A graduate of Wheaton College, *Time* once named him one of "The 25 Most Influential Evangelicals in America." Gerson correctly captures the inability of Republicans to urge voters choose the lesser of two evils.

"Here is the problem in sum: Republicans have not been given the option of choosing the lesser of two evils," Gerson wrote. "The GOP has selected someone who is unfit to be president, lacking the temperament, stability, judgment and compassion to occupy the office.

This is a terrible error, which has probably cost conservatives a majority on the Supreme Court. But the mistake was made by Republican primary voters in choosing Trump—not by those who can't, in good conscience, support him."[68]

Given Trump's racist, vulgar, unjust, violent, uncompassionate, and grotesque rhetoric and policy proposals, conservative Christians cannot in good faith call him the "lesser of two evils." Fear and hatred of Clinton doesn't justify supporting Trump. He's morally far beyond what pastors and Christian leaders can embrace. We must not yoke ourselves to a godless strongman who in nearly every way reflects the opposite values and attitudes of our Lord.

VOTE YOUR CONSCIENCE

Man I saw at a Donald Trump rally in Iowa in 2016.

Seems like good year to just say "no" in the ballot box.

Chapter 3: Don't Sell Ya Soul

I first heard Donald Trump speak in 2011 at a conservative Christian political event. In the 2012 afterward to the paperback edition of my book on religious rhetoric in presidential campaigns,[1] I noted his speech to show that even a vulgar, thrice-married casino mogul like Trump could use religious rhetoric to win votes in a presidential election. I'm both a little proud and quite scared by my prophetic insights! As he had during multiple previous presidential elections, Trump flirted in 2011 with running. Although he decided against it, the media attention he garnered with the striptease helped him as he prepped for running four years later. Ralph Reed, former leader of the Christian Coalition, also helped Trump that year by inviting him to serve as the keynote speaker for the annual meeting of Reed's new group, the Faith & Freedom Coalition (FFC). I attended the FFC and reported on it for *Ethics Daily*.[2] Nothing that weekend compared to the spectacle of Trump and the raucous reaction the crowd of conservative Christians gave him. Reed even boasted tickets skyrocketed after adding Trump to the program. As speakers blared the O'Jays song "For the Love of Money," a triumphant Trump waltzed up the stairs and waved to the cheering crowd.

"Money, money, money, money, money," declares the song, which served as the theme music for Trump's TV show *The Apprentice*.

Trump started his speech by showing a picture of his childhood confirmation class at First Presbyterian Church in Jamaica, New York.[3] He held up a copy of the picture as the image was also displayed on the large video screens—as if he needed to prove he had been in the class. During his flirtation with a presidential run earlier that year, Trump focused primarily on demanding yet more evidence from President Barack Obama that Obama was indeed born in Hawaii. After Obama released the long-form version of his birth certificate, Trump's popularity in presidential polling collapsed and he soon dropped out to instead host another season of his reality TV show.

"Good, right?" Trump said after showing the photo of his confirmation class. "That doesn't always play, but in this crowd it plays."

Trump then quickly left any discussion of religion or religious topics and did not provide any evidence of religious behavior during his adult life. Yet, in that moment of brutal honesty, he made an important admission: he knew that crowd of conservative Christians was susceptible to religious-political pandering. Even Trump could pull it off. This concerned me then—even more so now.

"As Trump's popularity at the FFC conference suggests, being Republican—rather than faithful—seemed to be the prerequisite for the event that included dozens of Republican politicians among the speakers," I wrote in my 2011 *Ethics Daily* piece. "Trump's star power and harsh attacks on Obama seemed to allow many of the conservative evangelicals at the event to overlook his past moral failings."

As the sound of "money, money, money, money, money" once again filled the room, Trump shook hands with Reed and left the stage to yet another standing ovation. The music cut away, however, before the lyrics shifted from the "money" refrain to how "the love of money" causes people to "steal," "lie," and "cheat."

"I know that money is the root of all evil," the O'Jays say. "Don't sell ya soul for the money—no no."

At the time, the Trump appearance and reception bothered me, but I figured he couldn't make things worse. Like most people, I was wrong! Trump started dipping his toe in the campaign waters again. But this time he actually ran. As in 2011, he showed an ability to win cheers from many conservative evangelicals as he utilized inflammatory rhetoric and awkwardly tried to prove some religious credentials. It seems like a farce, and yet he still borrowed pages from the religious playbook of the last few decades of presidential politicking. We've clearly reached a point where the sacred can be exploited by the profane. As with Trump's deceptive editing of the O'Jays song, it seems we cheer one line out of context while ignoring the clear biblical truths. We take moral critiques and twist them around to justify supporting Trump. This isn't a reality TV show for our entertainment. This is our gospel witness at stake.

I first saw Hillary Clinton speak during the 2008 presidential campaign. She showed up at a meeting of African-American Baptists in Georgia shortly before the Peach State primary. Barack Obama appeared via video and received a much more thunderous reception. As she has on numerous occasions, she talked about her Methodist faith and background.

"Much like all of you, I was taught from a very early age that my faith carried with it certain obligations," she said after noting her status as a Methodist and Bill's Baptist background. "I have been a praying person, luckily, my entire life. I'm often asked whether or not I am. I am quick to tell people that I was raised by parents who were prayerful and by a church that guided me but had I not been a praying person, one week in the White House would've turned me into a praying person."[4]

After quoting scriptures and talking about her faith, she launched into an attack of President George W. Bush's administration (although she didn't mention his name). She accused Bush of a "betrayal" of "the values of our faith." Clinton also used religious imagery to describe her political goals, perhaps mixing the two so that her politics becomes the work of God. She pledged to bring people to "the table in God's household." God's table, however, isn't found at 1600 Pennsylvania Avenue and definitely not at the Democratic Party's headquarters. She then moved into a typical campaign speech, listing her various policies proposals. Shortly after the halfway point of her speech, references to faith or scriptures disappeared. At that point she might as well have been speaking to a secular gathering. This was about winning votes, not offering spiritual edification or inspiration.

I worried about the presentations from Obama and Clinton since those two held goals in contrast to the rest of the gathering. Clinton and Obama sought votes. The Baptist pastors sought religious unity across denominational lines and ways to minister together. Neither candidate was Baptist and no Republican spoke, thus making it seem partisan politics trumped faith. To be fair, a leader of the gathering said all presidential candidates from both parties were invited. The fact that Republican candidates didn't attend is troubling as they ignore African-American Christians, but it could also be that they viewed the group as heavily Democratic and therefore not worth the time. When we align ourselves with just one party, we risk making it seem we're making spiritual judgments based on partisan affiliation. And we lose the chance to prophetically speak truth to power as we seek access from one side and are dismissed as partisan hacks by the other.

Did Evangelicals Really Vote for Trump?

The 2016 Republican primary process already hurt our Christian witness and I fear the general election campaign could do even more damage. In addition to high-profile Christian leaders who endorsed Trump during the primaries, much media coverage highlighted Trump's successes with evangelicals in the primary elections. Of the 17 Republican candidates, none stood further from the values conservative evangelicals claim to profess. Yet, none garnered more evangelical voters than Trump. Apparently little separates conservative evangelicals from conservatives in general. We've become Republicans (or Democrats) first and Christians second. Washington, D.C., Hollywood, and New York City do more to shape our worldviews and values than Jerusalem, Bethlehem, and Sinai. If being Christian doesn't make us different, we're doing it wrong.

I should note a couple important caveats that most media outlets ignored in their coverage of Trump and evangelicals during the primaries. His support was not as broad or deep as often portrayed. Trump merely won a plurality of evangelicals (not a majority). That means he won more than other candidates but most evangelicals still voted for someone else. Of the 26 states with exit polling data, the only states where Trump won a majority of evangelicals (Connecticut, Pennsylvania, Maryland, and Indiana) came at the very end as his delegate lead became virtually insurmountable. His overall vote total—not just support from evangelicals—also skyrocketed in those states as people fell in line and joined the winning team. Meanwhile, a majority of evangelicals in three states (Texas, Missouri, and Wisconsin) actually backed a candidate (Senator Ted Cruz) earlier during the contested part of the campaign, which is particularly interesting in Missouri where Trump won the overall vote even as he lost evangelicals. Overall in the 26 states, Trump won about 37.9 percent of evangelicals, nudging past Cruz's 34.8 percent. That means, however, that more than 62 percent of self-identified evangelicals voted for a candidate not named "Trump."

A second caveat: among Christians who actually attend church services weekly or more, Trump's support collapsed (usually going to Cruz). Trump dominated among Christians who claim the title and yet often don't attend church. This trend emerged in Reuters polling and in exit polls in the only two states (Missouri and Indiana) where Republican voters were asked about how frequently they attended religious services. Using church attendance as a filter—instead of self-identification as an evangelical—may suggest a critical divide between those who merely feel a cultural affinity with a religious identity from those who actively embrace the religious life. Bob Perry, a longtime church health consultant and author, said he feared the term "evangelical" was being hurt by "the highly politicized environment of an election year."[5]

"It is now a political word being thrown around by politicians and pundits who have no clear idea of the origin of the word or an accurate definition of it," he explained. "One can now see 'evangelicals' whose values and behavior show no semblance to the gospel and no conformity to the teachings of Jesus. There have long been 'cultural evangelicals' who identified themselves with the religious traditions of their parents or grandparents. Now we have 'political evangelicals' for whom arrogance is preferred over humility, material success is preferred over generosity of spirit, hateful speech is preferred over kindness, and spectacle is preferred over dignity. God forgive us."[6]

Adding to this difference based on church attendance is a third caveat: there also emerged a regional evangelical divide. Of the two regions of the country where evangelicals make up most of the Republican electorate—the Deep South and the Midwest—we saw divergent results. Trump won huge in the Deep South, dominating evangelicals in South Carolina, Georgia, Alabama, Mississippi, Florida, Tennessee, and Virginia. He also won evangelicals in New England, but those states included few evangelical voters. In the 26 states with exit poll data, he only captured a plurality of evangelicals in 17 states: seven in the Deep South, seven in New England, and three others (Nevada, Michigan, and Indiana). Of the remaining nine states with exit polling data, Trump lost North Carolina, Ohio and then a massive wall of states in the Midwest that runs from Mexico to Canada (Texas, Oklahoma, Arkansas, Missouri, Illinois, Iowa, and Wisconsin). Only two states—Arkansas and Missouri—saw evangelicals break with the overall winner of their state (as evangelicals in those two states went with Cruz while Trump won the overall vote). In a few other states without exit polls, we can guess if Trump won evangelical support or not based on the overall voting data. Consider the map below I created, which shows Trump wins among evangelicals in light gray and Trump losses among evangelicals in black (and states in white are where we don't have enough data or that voted after Trump garnered the nomination).

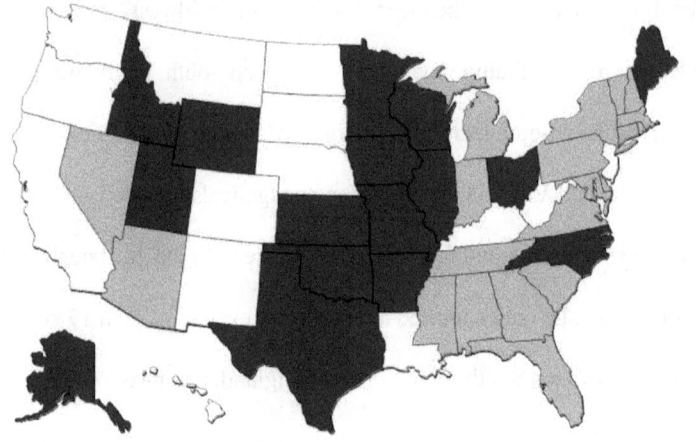

Scott Lamb, a graduate of Southern Baptist Theological Seminary and author of the 2015 authorized biography of Huckabee,[7] sees regional differences at play in the voting trends.

"I think Midwest evangelicals (like those in my home state of Missouri) live in a 'border state' religious existence," he explained. "Go further South and you've got cultural reasons to be religious, the

'It's the right thing to do' or 'It's good for business' motivations for being churched. But as you get into border states, you've got less of that—not radically less mind you, but it's definitely not the Bible Belt mentality."[8]

Hal Bass, professor of political science at Ouachita Baptist University in Arkadelphia, Arkansas, and author of a book on U.S. political parties,[9] also thinks evangelicals may be taking on regional differences in voting habits. In essence, he thinks geography and culture are impacting the worldviews and politics of evangelicals more than theology. He argued that "any differentiation between Midwestern evangelicals and Southern evangelicals may well pertain more to the regional identity than to the evangelical one."[10] Thus, he thinks "it is questionable to assume that the evangelical label is the trigger for voting behavior."[11] One regional difference Bass noted—authoritarian—fits with what we saw about Trump and his supporters in the previous chapter.

"The South has long been considered strongly patriotic in its sentiments," Bass explained. "Trump's nationalistic commitment to make America great again resonates especially well in the region. ... Considerations of the Southern subculture have typically identified an authoritarian affinity. It is at least arguable that some aspects of evangelicalism also feature this authoritarian affinity. To the extent that Trump projects an image of strength, he taps into prevailing sentiments that look favorably on strong authority figures and may well trump, if you will, recognition of and concerns about his background and behavior."[12]

These three issues (plurality, church attendance, and regional differences) are important, but don't let evangelicals off the hook. Trump didn't win a majority of evangelicals, but he still did better than anyone else. That nearly 38 percent of evangelicals voted for him is not a cause for celebration, especially as his evangelical support topped 40 percent in 11 of the 26 states. Without this support, Trump wouldn't have garnered the nomination. In the 26 states, evangelicals accounted for 55.9 percent of the Republican voters. Trump couldn't have won the nomination without evangelicals. Trump recognizes that and frequently thanks "the evangelicals" for his win. I worry that every time Trump thanks "the evangelicals," another church dies (or an angel loses its wings). During his acceptance address at the Republican convention in July, Trump thanked evangelicals and then added—off-script—that he didn't deserve their support. Even he knows it! If only evangelicals knew it and stopped giving him support.

The church attendance and regional caveats are important, but also don't give us an excuse (although regular church attenders in the Midwest like myself feel at least a little bit better!). First, we see regional values holding greater sway on people than theology. That should set off alarm bells! Second, this means we have many people who view themselves as faithful followers even if they infrequently attend church. We've allowed a cultural affinity to substitute for an active faith. We've created a religious-political environment where a candidate can offer a few remarks about Jesus and then be backed as a godly choice. Interestingly, Jerry Falwell, Jr., one of Trump's top Christian proponents, even admits that evangelicals are now really not unique from Americans in general as cultural identifications trump religious concerns.

"There were times in our past that evangelicals were defined by this or that social issue," Falwell said shortly before speaking at the Republican convention to urge votes for Trump. "We're at a point now when evangelicals are just Americans, just like every other group you can think of."[13]

If our faith doesn't make us different, then that's quite a condemnation of our churches. We've watered down the term "evangelical" and now it's haunting us. Russell Moore of the Southern

Baptist Convention's Ethics & Religious Liberty Commission and one of the top evangelical voices against Trump in this campaign even penned a *Washington Post* column in February about how he likes to call himself a "gospel Christian" now instead of an "evangelical" because of "this crazy campaign year."[14]

"The word 'evangelical' has become almost meaningless this year, and in many ways the word itself is at the moment subverting the gospel of Jesus Christ,"[15] he added.

Moore captured the problem well. It's not the loss of the term "evangelical" that is the issue, but that it hurts our gospel witness. It allows journalists, pundits, and politicians to create a narrative of Trump as the Christian candidate. May God forgive us! We must not allow this problem to grow in the general election by lending our support to Trump. If we do, this campaign will leave scars on our public witness that'll take years—if not a generation lost in the wilderness—to overcome.

The Democratic primaries brought less information about the role of religion, in large part due to exit pollsters and journalists heavily focusing their attention on evangelical Republican voting trends. Democrats weren't ever asked if they were evangelicals even though more than twenty percent of white evangelicals consistently vote

Democratic and an even greater percentage of non-white evangelicals do. In some states Democrats received questions about religious affiliation and/or about religious attendance rates. In only two of 27 states where exit polling data exists for Democratic voters were those voters asked about their religious affiliation (Florida and New York). Both showed little differences between Catholics and Protestants, but showed Clinton easily winning those claiming a religious affiliation and Sanders winning those who claimed "none" when asked. Considering Sanders is a nonobservant Jew who did much better with younger voters (who are more likely to claim "none"), the results aren't surprising.

Additionally, in eight Southern states exit pollsters asked Democrats about how frequently they attend religious services. The more someone attended church, the more likely they were to back Clinton. But she easily won all eight of those states and the states are all in the same region so the findings aren't that helpful. When someone wins a state by a large margin, they tend to win nearly all demographic groups, so the findings in these blowout states aren't necessarily insightful. What about regular church attenders in the Midwest or in states where Sanders easily won? We don't know what differences may have emerged. What the results largely tell us is that southern African-American church attenders strongly backed Clinton—just as southern African-American voters in general did. The results also show how little exit pollsters and the news organizations who help write the exit poll questions understand about religion. Faith is being reduced to something evangelical Republicans or southern African-American Democrats care about, but little else. But even with little data we see a few hints in the Democratic results that mirror the Republican ones: electoral decisions are more impacted by other factors (age, race, geography, etc.) than by religion. Clergy across the theological and political spectrums should be concerned by the exit poll data.

Two Corinthians … Walk into a Casino Bar

Throughout the 2016 presidential campaign, evangelist Franklin Graham is traveling across the country holding large rallies at state capitol buildings. I attended the Missouri rally of his 50-state "Decision America 2016 Tour." Taking advantage of the political election, Graham's stump speech at the capitols during the tour hits several political messages. He bills this as a nonpartisan speech, and offers a few lines in that direction. He even changed his party affiliation from 'Republican' to 'Independent' before kicking off the tour (although that former affiliation shows his general partisan leaning).

"I have zero hope in the Democratic Party," he declared. "I have zero hope in the Republican Party. The only hope for this country is Almighty God."

Yet, Graham wasn't being apolitical as he still urged people to vote. In fact, he implied it would be wrong to not vote. Thus, he urged the crowd to vote and pray for politicians so that "God will use them for his glory."

"In this next election, I want you to vote," Graham declared. "I'm not here today to tell you who to vote for. It's not about Republicans or Democrats. ... You might have to go the polls and hold your nose. You might have to vote for the least of the two heathens."

One of Graham's key priorities in the speech came as he made a pitch for identity politics by arguing we should vote for Christians. He actually focused more time on urging we get more Christians in office (especially for local school boards) than he spent addressing issues and principles. He urged each Christian to "be a community organizer for God" and "be a political activist for God."

"I want you to get involved in the political process," Graham said. "Some of you can go out and run for office. ... We need Christians on the school boards. We need Christian mayors, we need Christian city councils, we need Christian county commissioners."

Graham's identity politics argument surprised me since I don't think he actually agrees with that philosophy. After all, he publicly backed Republican Mitt Romney (a Mormon) for president over Democrat Barack Obama (a Christian) in 2012. Of course, Graham inaccurately and disgracefully suggested Obama is a Muslim, so perhaps that's how he tries to justify his vote. Regardless what one thinks of Obama politically, he's been very clear and articulate in expressing his personal faith in Jesus. Espousing identity politics as a priority would also lead Graham to back Clinton over Trump, since she's likely the only Christian of the two (and since he said pick one of the two). One can reject Clinton's politics, but she's been quite consistent and articulate about her Methodist beliefs. I don't think Graham will actually back Clinton as he's praised Trump's presidential potential in the past.[16] But let's be very clear: Trump cannot be called "a Christian" in any orthodox sense. As Russell Moore of the Southern Baptist Convention put it, Trump is a "lost person" who needs to "repent of sin and come to faith in Jesus Christ."[17] I echo this not merely because of his sexual exploits, his business corruption, his racism, or other problems explored in the previous chapter. While his behavior and rhetoric do not show evidence of him transforming into a new creation, we really don't need to look any further than his own words about God, Jesus, and salvation.

Early in the presidential campaign, Trump spoke at the Family Leadership Summit in Ames, Iowa, sponsored by conservative Christian groups like the Family Research Council and Liberty University. Moderator Frank Luntz asked Trump if he'd ever asked God for forgiveness. That's the equivalent of a softball at a religious gathering, but somehow Trump still whiffed. He not only denied his need to ask for forgiveness—a core biblical concept—but also managed to mock communion.

"I am not sure I have," Trump said. "I just go on and try to do a better job from there. I don't think so. I think if I do something wrong, I think, I just try and make it right. I don't bring God into that picture. I don't."[18]

"When I drink my little wine—which is about the only wine I drink—and have my little cracker, I guess that is a form of asking for forgiveness, and I do that as often as possible because I feel cleansed," he added. "I think in terms of 'let's go on and let's make it right.'"[19]

Anyone who thinks they don't need to ask God for forgiveness and can instead just make everything right all by themselves cannot, in good faith, be called "a Christian." Trump echoed his lack of need for forgiveness in a later interview. Then when asked on another occasion to name his favorite Bible verse, he went for "an eye for an eye" out of the Old Testament (I explore this answer more in appendix three). That's an incredibly odd verse to be inspired by! So many passages on love and grace and mercy and he goes with gouging out someone's eye in revenge? As if the verse itself wasn't problematic enough to be called one's favorite, it's a verse that Jesus himself literally argued against. In the 'Sermon on the Mount,' Jesus replaced the 'eye for eye' ethical code with a new commandment to turn the other cheek and go the extra mile. It's almost like Trump started reading the Bible for the campaign and hadn't made it to the New Testament yet!

Then in June of 2016, conservative columnist Cal Thomas returned to the subject of forgiveness and framed the question quite clearly: "You have said you never felt the need to ask for God's forgiveness, and yet repentance for one's sins is a precondition to salvation. I ask you the question Jesus asked of Peter: Who do you say he is?"[20] Perhaps because Thomas explicitly called seeking repentance as "a precondition to salvation," Trump changed his answer a bit.

"I will be asking for forgiveness, but hopefully I won't have to be asking for much forgiveness," Trump said. "As you know, I am Presbyterian and Protestant. I've had great relationships and developed even greater relationships with ministers. We have tremendous support from the clergy. I think I will be doing very well during the election with evangelicals and with Christians."[21]

Trump then went on to talk about Middle East policies to attack Obama. But notice what he didn't do in his answer. He didn't say who he thought Jesus is. He made the awkward and redundant claim he's "Presbyterian and Protestant" and then switched to talk about electoral success. He's defining his religious beliefs by how many votes he won, as if clergy endorsements for his presidential campaign are transferrable to vouch for his salvation if anyone raises questions at the pearly gates. As a sharp interviewer, Thomas also noticed Trump didn't actually answer the question. So Thomas again asked, "Who do you say Jesus is?"[22]

"Jesus to me is somebody I can think about for security and confidence," Trump said. "Somebody I can revere in terms of bravery and in terms of courage and, because I consider the Christian religion so important, somebody I can totally rely on in my own mind."[23]

That's a far cry from Peter's famous declaration to the same question: "You are the Messiah, the Son of the living God."[24] Trump's answer reads like some 'new age' doublespeak about meditating on Jesus in his head but letting the influence go no further. He seems to view Jesus as some lucky charm a gambler takes into one of Trump's casinos. If I close my eyes and think about Jesus while the roulette wheel spins, then perhaps he'll give me the security and confidence I need to land red. If I rely on Jesus in my own mind enough, maybe he'll even give me the bravery and courage to try a round of blackjack.

Trump's "faith" ultimately seems to be what Jesus called "Mammon." Trump's strongest support from pastors during the primaries came from 'prosperity' gospel preachers. It makes sense that he likes them and they like him. The 'prosperity gospel' preaches that wealth is a sign of God's blessing. These 'preachers' often urge you to give to their ministry to prove your faith and to sow your seed that will supposedly spark God to give you more in return. Trump returned the favor to them by having three 'prosperity gospel' preachers at the microphone during his nominating convention. He then did the normal practice of having lots of interfaith diversity as his convention included two Catholics, one fundamentalist Christian (Falwell), one mainline Protestant, one Greek Orthodox, one Mormon, one Jew, one Sikh, and one Muslim. Trump's faith is that of the 'prosperity gospel,' which really isn't the gospel. We really don't need to look any further than the warning from Paul to Timothy to avoid those who "who have been robbed of the truth and who think that godliness is a means to financial gain."[25]

"For we brought nothing into the world, and we can take nothing out of it," Paul added. "But if we have food and clothing, we will be content with that. Those who want to get rich fall into temptation and a trap and into many foolish and harmful desires that plunge people into ruin and destruction. For the love of money is a root of all kinds of evil. Some people, eager for money, have wandered from the faith and pierced themselves with many griefs."[26]

Despite all of that, some preachers still try to sanctify Trump, contorting the scriptures into an unrecognizable tale of power over piety, ego over ethics, party over principles, commodities over conscience. When Jerry Falwell, Jr. introduced Trump at Liberty University in January of 2016, he compared Trump to Jesus and Martin Luther King, Jr. He called Trump "a breath of fresh air" who "speaks the plain commonsense truth."[27] He even cited scriptures to praise Trump's character.

"Matthew 7:16 tells us that by their fruits you shall know them," Falwell said. "Donald Trump's life has borne fruit, fruit that has provided jobs to multitudes of people in addition to the many he has helped with his generosity. ... I have seen firsthand that his staff loves him and is loyal to him because of his servant leadership. In my opinion Donald Trump lives a life of loving and helping others as Jesus taught in the great commandment."

Trump's speech at Liberty University, by the way, is the one where Trump showed his biblical familiarity by reading a verse from "Two Corinthians" (I guess two Corinthians are better than one!). Or consider what former Christian Coalition leader Ralph Reed said after hosting Trump at his 2016 Faith and Freedom Coalition event.

"I think if you look at the things that we, as conservative evangelicals believe in—life, marriage, religious freedom, support for Israel, and terrorism—I think Donald Trump stands for the positions that advance the good,"[28] Reed claimed, apparently with a straight face.

Trump remains untrustworthy on many of those issues, but let's focus just on the second one. Marriage? Trump does believe in marriage, but not in the way evangelicals do. He treats it like a short-term investment one can dump and move on—almost as if he's merely filing bankruptcy for yet another company so he can focus on his new project. It's not just that he's been divorced twice—it's that he's openly boasted about cheating and used vulgar language to publicly fantasize about others with whom he'd like to cheat. Reed and others preach against the "redefining of marriage," but nothing compares to the word distortions of making Trump a believer in traditional marriage values. At some point I start to view Reed with the same credibility as the priest in *The Princess Bride*: "Mawwiage, that bwessed awwangement, that dweam within a dweam. And wove, twue wove." Others sadly make Reed's remarks not look so bad in comparison. After a meeting between Trump and conservative Christian pastors and leaders, Marjorie Danenfelser of the Susan B. Anthony List even defined Trump as one of them.

"I believe that he came across very well as a messenger for everybody in the room, not just as a beneficiary of evangelical votes but as a fellow traveler,"[29] she said.

I'm not sure what trip she and Trump are on, but it's hardly evangelical! Even worse, shortly after James Dobson joined Trump's evangelical advisory board (designed to help Trump win evangelical votes in November), Dobson decided to forcibly plunge Trump into the baptismal waters by claiming Trump's now a Christian.

"He did accept a relationship with Christ," Dobson claimed in June. "I know the person who led him to Christ, and that's fairly recent. ... I believe he really made a commitment, but he's a baby Christian."[30]

Dobson then excused Trump's vulgarity (as Trump cursed during a meeting with Dobson and about 1,000 Christian pastors and leaders) by saying Trump's still learning. If Dobson thinks we need a Christian leader as president—and thus Trump needs to get saved—a "baby Christian" hardly counts as a Christian *leader*. Even worse, Dobson later said the person who supposedly led this conversion was 'prosperity gospel' preacher Paula White, who proclaims a gospel closer to the life of Trump than Jesus. And to be clear, garnering the Republican nomination doesn't count as a born-again conversion. Dobson later walked back the comments, but still suggested Trump might be saved and urged Christians to vote for Trump. If someone plans to vote for Trump because he's a good Christian candidate, then they're either not paying attention to Trump in the news or not paying attention to Jesus in the Bible. If only there was a biblical proverb to warn Dobson and other evangelical leaders who sat down with Trump and gobbled up his politics.

When you sit to dine with a ruler, note well what is before you,

and put a knife to your throat if you are given to gluttony.

Do not crave his delicacies, for that food is deceptive.[31]

A New Identity

Trump's lack of salvation experience ultimately doesn't matter to my vote. I reject Franklin Graham's idea of identity politics. Thus, I will not vote for Hillary Clinton merely because she's the more committed Christian of the two. So let's address this issue clearly: should we vote for the Christian candidate? This is, after all, the basic driving belief behind the expectation that presidential candidates openly talk about their faith and come speak to our churches. Clinton and Trump go to churches on the campaign trail, quote scripture, and have pastors pray at the start of rallies all to try to prove their religious credentials. Campaign advisors know the candidates need to show religiosity to win over some voters. We clap and vote for politicians who testify about their beliefs because we seem to think being a Christian will make someone a better president or senator or school board member. But is that actually true?

Did you pick your doctor because they're a Christian, or were you more concerned about if they'd been to medical school, are covered by your insurance, and are well reviewed by others? What about a financial advisor or a car mechanic or a chef? While I want to make sure these individuals act ethically and fairly, they don't have to be a Christian to get my business. I'm more concerned about do they have the training and skills necessary to do the job well. We should treat a job like U.S. president much the same. We need leaders who are ethical (and I think Trump and Clinton both fall short in that regard), but there are good, moral people who aren't Christians. I wouldn't pick such persons for a church leadership position, but I'm fine with them in other areas of leadership. For our nation's leaders, we need people who are skilled and trained to do the job well. The godliest, most righteous Christians aren't probably prepping themselves with such skills as they're instead involved in serving the Kingdom. Some Christian groups (like the Mennonites) even historically discouraged believers from serving in governmental positions. My criteria for picking a pastor remains quite different from picking a president.

The idea of identity politics runs counter to the spirit of our 'founding fathers.' The only religious reference in the original text of the U.S. Constitution is a prohibition against the use of religious tests for office. Expecting someone to profess Christianity before we vote for them hurts democracy and religion. It hurts our democracy as we essentially disenfranchise many people from full citizenship and, more importantly, it hurts Christianity as some politicians will fake it just to gain power.

I mention these issues of identity politics and Trump's lack of Christian commitment not to urge a vote against Trump (I offered my real reasons in the previous chapter). Instead, it helps us see two things. First, it shows us the absurdity of pastors and Christian leaders who attempt to sanctify Trump. They do it since they're working on this problematic ground of identity politics. So they twist biblical teachings around to bless Trump. That's reading the Bible through the lens of politics instead of the other way around. These pastors and Christian leaders must be critiqued and urged to repent. If someone tells you to vote for Trump because he's a godly person, reject that person as a false prophet. Similarly, if someone tells you to vote for Clinton because she's a godly person, tell them we must instead judge candidates on the issues and merits.

Second, Trump in this campaign showed the problem of our political expectations that candidates talk about their faith (as we'll explore more in the next chapter). It turns out that can be faked—even by a vulgar thrice-married casino mogul with ties to mobsters and racists. It's okay to elect a nonbeliever. Thomas Jefferson, the writer of the Declaration of Independence, consistently sits near the top of the lists of greatest presidents. Yet, he was perhaps the least Christian president in our nation's history. Jefferson famously cut out all the parts of the New Testament he disagreed with (like the miracles of Jesus). Perhaps instead of using altar calls as political auditions we should instead evaluate candidates based on their ideas, experience, and ethics. If the best candidate is a believer, then great. We can vote for them and pray for them in office. But if the best candidate doesn't share our religious beliefs, we can vote for them and pray for them in office—and pray for their salvation as well!

Given the abuses of religious rhetoric in politics, perhaps it's time to ask our candidates to quit talking about God. We might find this advice a bit tough to swallow, but I think ultimately it will help us disentangle our churches from our political parties. Perhaps we'll stop inviting them to speak at our religious gatherings and stop clapping when they use holy scriptures (usually out of context) to pander to us. Maybe it'll help us to quit thinking we can "save our nation" or "take back our nation for God" by electing the right politician to sit in the White house. Revival won't come from ballot boxes or conquering crusades. It requires prophets, not politicians. We already have a savior and he's not on the ballot because he's our Lord and King with no term limits or need for a mandate from the people.

"No King But Jesus." Amen!

Saw these signs abandoned inside Missouri Capitol during Franklin Graham's rally.

VOTE YOUR CONSCIENCE

Chapter 4: Victory in Jesus?

During a trip in April to meet with Baptists in eastern Cuba (mentioned in more detail in appendix five), I had a stopover in the Turks & Caicos Islands (I figure if someone needs to serve God in the Caribbean it might as well be me!). Our team took a cab ride to find a restaurant and see a bit of the island. During the short ride, one of the members called me "kid" since I was 25-30 years younger than the other five members in the group. I quickly responded, "Hey, as of this year I'm old enough to run for president!" Without missing a beat and before anyone else on the team could respond, our cab driver—a native of the Turks & Caicos—responded, "Might as well." That seems like a pretty good assessment of the 2016 campaign.

For members of my generation, evangelical Christianity and partisan politics have always been tightly wrapped together. That wasn't always the case. But in the late 1970s and early 1980s, several evangelical leaders succeeded in aligning the faith closely with the Republican Party. That means that for my whole life it's seemed as if GOP stood for "God's Only Party." Some pastors basically act that way as they depict voting for a Democrat to be a sin (and some liberal pastors basically make the opposite argument). Making Christianity just another partisan political tool, however, has hurt our churches. It's one reason many in my generation are turned off from churches, preferring instead to call themselves "spiritual but not religious." For our entire lives the church has seemed like another political special interest group or even a wing of one party.

Scholars Robert Putnam (professor of public policy at Harvard University) and David Campbell (professor of political science at the University of Notre Dame) interviewed thousands of Americans over multiple years as they researched and wrote their award-winning book *American Grace: How Religion Divides and Unites Us*.[1] It's a good book, and I've talked in person with Putnam as he explained key findings on one big reason Millennials and other younger Americans are leaving churches. They note the rise of the "nones" (those who claim "none" when asked their religious affiliation), but stress these "nones" aren't atheists.

"[T]hey have been alienated from organized religion by its increasingly conservative politics," the two authors wrote in a column. "This backlash was especially forceful among youth coming of age in the 1990s and just forming their views about religion."[2]

"Political allegiances and religious observance became more closely aligned, and both religion and politics became more polarized," they added, "Increasingly, young people saw religion as intolerant, hypocritical, judgmental and homophobic. If being religious entailed political conservatism, they concluded, religion was not for them."[3]

As I noted in chapter one, the ice cream sure can be messed up when mixed with manure. We are losing much of a generation in part due to aligning our faith too closely with one partisan party. I recognize there are other factors (I lead the 'generational engagement team' for a statewide Baptist network, which means I work with churches as they seek to reach younger generations like my fellow Millennials). But partisan politics is a big reason churches are losing Millennials and one we could easily have avoided. Making Christian churches—especially white evangelical ones—an extension of the Republican Party means we're putting the credibility of our churches in the hands of politicians. When they fall, we suffer. When they lie, get caught in a sexual scandal, get indicted, or lie and flip-flop, closely-aligned churches get a new dent. We have enough scandals and problems of our own to overcome. I'm not suggesting we water down the gospel just to pack the pews. But what we've done with partisan politics is water down the gospel and drive people away! The marriage with the Republican Party produced little for us, though it helped them win some elections. The remains true for liberal Christians who aligned themselves with the

Democratic Party. Rather than winning our nation for Christ—as some partisan preachers claimed we would—we've instead sent the culture spiraling in the opposite direction. As we transformed ourselves into chaplains for a political empire, we washed away much of our saltiness and turned down the dimmer switch on our light.

The most troubling part of Putnam and Campbell's research comes in realizing what happens when politics and church collide. It used to be that if one's political party and one's church came into conflict, one would most likely change politics or even party. Now, the reverse is usually true as Americans have "adjusted their religion to fit their politics."[4]

"We were initially skeptical about that proposition, because it seemed implausible that people would make choices that might affect their eternal fate based on how they felt about George W. Bush," the scholars wrote. "But the evidence convinced us that many Americans now are sorting themselves out on Sunday morning on the basis of their political views."[5]

Did you catch that? If someone's chosen political party offers an opinion contrary to the teachings of their church, that person is more likely to just change churches. Thus, we end up with red churches and blue churches as we segregate based on political differences. If people are more likely to change churches than parties, that means our political parties hold greater sway over the minds and even souls of those in our pews (and perhaps even behind our pulpits). More often than not, people are pledging greater allegiance to partisan politics. When Christians view religion through the lens of politics (instead of the other way around), we've lost sight of our mission. Former U.S. Senator John Danforth, a Republican who is also an Episcopalian priest, captured the problem well.

"We have a strong inclination to let our politics determine our faith rather than the other way around," he lamented. "When we vest our personal opinions with the trappings of religion, we make religion the servant of our politics. By confusing faith and politics, we become transformed to this world."[6]

How Did We Get Here?

Christianity—even evangelical Christianity—didn't always necessarily mean one voted Republican. Things started changing in the 1970s. By the end of the 1980s, Christianity (especially evangelical Christianity) would be viewed by many as merely a branch of the Republican Party. Diversity still exists with devout Christians found in the Republican Party, Democratic Party, Libertarian Party, Green Party, and many others. But the public image of Christianity as aligned with one political party is a particularly contemporary problem. Polling data reveals that until 1972, no significant partisan voting difference existed between those who attended church frequently and those who did not. Now this so-called "God gap" stands as one of the main electoral differences between the two major parties—even when Democrats nominate a candidate who attends church much more frequently than the Republican nominee. Thus, this "God gap" is tracked by political strategists as a key indicator of electoral success. Political operatives may now spend as much energy tracking if people show up to church as pastors and denominational leaders!

Several factors led to this religious-political shift in U.S. politics (and I explored them in more detail in my book on religious rhetoric in presidential campaigns[7]). The most significant shift, however came in the 1960s and 1970s as evangelical Protestants (like Southern Baptist, Assembly of God, and nondenominational churches) surpassed mainline Protestants (like Episcopal, Presbyterian, and Lutheran churches) as the largest religious group in the United States. A key marker of this shift occurred in 1967 as the Southern Baptist Convention (evangelical) overtook the United Methodist Church (mainline) as the largest Protestant denomination in the nation. While only four of the first 38 presidents were evangelicals, five of the most recent six could be designated as such (with only George H. W. Bush not fitting that description). Barack Obama shies away from using the term "evangelical" because of its connotation with conservative partisan politics, but the way he talks about God, the Bible, and his personal faith is clearly evangelical (which should not be surprising as the African-American Christian tradition is often highly evangelical).

This emergence of evangelicals as the largest faith group in the U.S. brought more attention to evangelicals. If someone can win a majority of the biggest group, then that offers a strategic advantage on election day. Size brought more media attention and more campaign contributions to groups promising to mobilize evangelicals. When journalists talk about religious voters in elections today, they often just mean white evangelical voters—as seen with the 2016 primary exit polls that focused almost entirely on tracking Republican evangelicals. Such lopsided data skewed coverage of the religious influence on the campaign and made it seem that only evangelicals mattered politically. White evangelicals remain one of the most partisan religious groups (consistently voting overwhelmingly Republican), so focusing media attention on them helps depict Christianity overall as closely aligned with one party even though African-American Christians vote overwhelmingly Democratic, mainline Protestants only slightly favor Republicans, and Catholics are usually closely split.

Courting Court Prophets

This rise of evangelicals as the largest religious group in the U.S. also brought a temptation to evangelicals to flex their political power. As the new largest religious demographic, evangelicals could shift from preaching from the margins and start ruling from the center. Electoral size and strength brings importance as politicians seek voting blocs. That brings access as many evangelical leaders involved in partisan politics soon discovered with White House invitations and special conference calls with top officials. That access, however, remains predicated on two factors: keep delivering results and be a good team player. The latter expectation particularly works to mute our prophetic voice. It's a temptation that haunts God's followers throughout history. The ancient kings of Israel acted with the same political desires as our contemporary politicians. The kings would employ "court prophets" to give them advice (like will God help me win if I decide to start a war with those people over there). Criticizing a king could result in you losing your job—or your head! Jeremiah condemned such false preachers for merely telling the king what he hoped to hear.

"From the least to the greatest, all are greedy for gain," Jeremiah proclaimed as he recited the words of God. "Prophets and priests alike, all practice deceit. They dress the wounds of my people as though it were not serious. 'Peace, peace,' they say when there is no peace. Are they ashamed of their detestable conduct? No, they have no shame at all; they do not even know how to blush."[8]

Jeremiah's divine warning could be reused today as preachers endorse Trump without blushing. Like the mythical Icarus, our pride leads us to fly too high until we lose our wings and come crashing down. It's the mistake Christians made by uniting their faith with Roman Emperor Constantine. Surely, many thought then, it's better to rule than be persecuted. And soon, they became the thing they once feared. Like in the end of George Orwell's *Animal Farm* when no one could tell a difference between the farmers and the pigs. We trade our conscience for a coalition, our altar for access. Too often the euphoria of election day gives way to broken promises and embarrassing scandals.

That ultimately is the biggest problem with how religious rhetoric is (mis)used in contemporary campaigns. As I documented in my research,[9] in every general election since 1976, the presidential nominee who talked the most about religion, scriptures, and faith won.

Every time! Jimmy Carter in 1976, Ronald Reagan in 1980 and 1984, George H. W. Bush in 1988, Bill Clinton in 1992 and 1996. George W. Bush in 2000 and 2004, and Barack Obama in 2008 and 2012. If that trend holds, it should worry Republicans since Hillary Clinton remains much more comfortable talking about her Methodist faith than Donald Trump does about religious matters (as we saw in the previous chapter). It's important to note, however, the winning presidents in those elections from 1976 through 2012 were those who talked the most about the Bible and Jesus—not necessarily those who were the most committed believers. Reagan rarely attended church but easily out-God-talked the Sunday School teacher he ran against in 1980.

This rhetorical religious expectation that our presidents talk about faith in a fairly evangelical manner represents a significant shift from earlier campaigns. John F. Kennedy won in 1960 in large part because he promised a group of Protestant clergy that he believed "the separation of church and state is absolute"[10] and that he wouldn't allow his own religious beliefs to trump his oath of office.

"I believe in a President whose religious views are his own private affair, neither imposed by him upon the nation or imposed by the nation upon him as a condition to holding that office," Kennedy added. "I would not look with favor upon a President working to subvert the First Amendment's guarantees of religious liberty."[11]

Kennedy's speech perfectly hit the tone people wanted to hear at the time and therefore helped him squeak out a narrow victory. Interestingly, the next Catholic to receive a major party's presidential nomination (John Kerry) found a much different religious-political environment 44 years later. While Kennedy faced criticism he was too Catholic/religious to be president, Kerry faced criticism he wasn't Catholic/religious enough. The irony? Kerry is a much more devout Catholic than Kennedy. It's not that Kerry was less religious but that societal expectations had changed. As a Northeastern Catholic, Kerry came from a tradition where one doesn't wear their religion on their sleeves. Thus, he struggled to speak publicly about his faith—especially compared to the evangelical George W. Bush.

Why does this matter? Politicians will do what it takes to win. If a candidate needs to have a Twitter account to win, they'll open it (and usually have a staffer write tweets—except Trump, of course). If they need to run TV ads to win, they'll spend millions on them. If they need to shake hands and kiss babies, they'll do it. And if they need to talk about Jesus and quote the Bible, they'll act like a preacher. That's why candidates like Trump who don't attend church (except for while running for office) will talk about church and faith. Rather than getting excited about politicians showing up in our churches and talking about Jesus, perhaps we should be skeptical, worried, and even (at least at times) upset. David Kuo, who served as a religious speechwriter for several politicians—including Jack Kemp, John Ashcroft, Bob Dole, and George W. Bush—came to regret using biblical verses and religious hymns for political purposes.

"This *should* have been driving me nuts," he wrote. "We were bastardizing God's words for our own political agenda and feeling good about it."[12]

When we make talking about Jesus a box to check on the way to the Oval Office, we invite the politicization of our faith. And that's exactly what's happened over the past few decades. Candidates aren't breaking into our churches; we're inviting them and then watching as the pastor steps aside and lets the politician have the pulpit. As the Okefenokee prophet Pogo said, "We have met the enemy and he is us." Thus, it's up to Christians to create prophetic distance. Tony Campolo urges us to "avoid the tendency to define *any* party as 'the God party.'"[13]

"We must take care as we get involved in politics, lest we fall victim to power's destructiveness," he added. "There is a great temptation to play power games and organize into a voting bloc, or even perhaps to create our own separate political party."[14]

A Dangerous Affair

Given how poorly the experiment of the past four decades has gone, perhaps we need a new political vision. My fellow white evangelicals have aligned ourselves to one partisan party, hurting our prophetic witness and our outreach to younger generations. Interestingly, evangelical leaders sometimes talk like they've learned that lesson. Back in 1998—two decades into the 'religious right' politicking and two years after Bill Clinton beat them for the second time—several conservative Christian leaders openly complained about how little they'd gained from the Republican Party. Gary Bauer, who at the time led the Family Research Council (and later ran for the 2000 Republican presidential nomination and now leads his own religious-political group American Values), lamented, "There is virtually nothing to show for an 18-year commitment."[15] Although Bauer supported Cruz in the primaries in 2016, he quickly fell in line behind Trump.

"The Republican Party and the conservative movement must be united," Bauer wrote the day Trump became the presumptive nominee. "We must defeat Hillary Clinton in November!"[16]

It's been 18 years since Bauer lamented having virtually nothing to show for an 18-year commitment. Now he lines up behind Trump. The effort seems to be heading into negative territory. In the same 1998 *New York Times* article in which Bauer complained, there was an even more telling remark. Richard Land, then-president of the Southern Baptist Convention's Ethics & Religious Liberty Commission (and now president of Southern Evangelical Seminary), offered quite a profane metaphor while complaining about how little evangelicals got from two decades of aligning with the Republican Party.

"The go-along, get-along strategy is dead," Land said. "No more engagement. We want a wedding ring, we want a ceremony, we want a consummation of the marriage."[17]

Wow. A Southern Baptist leader talking about how we evangelical Christians should pine for a secular political party to hop in bed with us and … well, that might be about what happened. Such an interesting claim considering it's the opposite argument many prophets made with the same basic metaphor. Prophet after prophet condemned the Hebrew people for being adulterous as they aligned themselves with other gods and nations.

"Have you seen what faithless Israel has done?" Jeremiah reported God asking. "She has gone up on every high hill and under every spreading tree and has committed adultery there."[18]

"See how the faithful city has become a prostitute!" Isaiah heard God say in a vision. "She once was full of justice; righteousness used to dwell in her—but now murderers!"[19]

"They defiled themselves by what they did," a poet cried out in Psalm 106, "by their deeds they prostituted themselves."[20]

"For you have been unfaithful to your God; you love the wages of a prostitute at every threshing floor,"[21] Hosea said God told him to tell Israel after God urged the prophet to live out the critique by marrying a prostitute who would cheat on him like Israel did to God.

"You took some of your garments to make gaudy high places, where you carried on your prostitution," Ezekiel noted God declared. "You went to him, and he possessed your beauty. …. You adulterous wife! You prefer strangers to your own husband! All prostitutes receive gifts, but you give gifts to all your lovers, bribing them to come to you from everywhere for your illicit favors. So in your prostitution you are the opposite of others; no one runs after you for your favors. You are the very opposite, for you give payment and none is given to you."[22]

God repeatedly used these sexual metaphors to critique the Hebrew people for not trusting in him and his rule. Yet, Land used the sexual metaphor to instead urge God's people to unite with the rulers of another kingdom! Land attacked Trump during the primaries—and criticized Christians who voted for him. But once we entered the general election phase of the campaign, he swept those concerns aside. Now Land is at Trump's service. Land insists he's going to "vote against Hillary Clinton and I don't believe in third party candidates" [23] (though they exist even if he doesn't believe in them). Thus, he urged Christians to vote for Trump over Clinton. Who are we willing to hop in bed with just because we hate Clinton? Land later joined Trump's evangelical advisory board, which is designed to help Trump win evangelical votes so he can become president. Interestingly, Land used to make an argument about marriage fidelity to blast candidates as unacceptable.

"[T]hree wives is one too many for most evangelical voters,"[24] Land said about Rudy Giuliani during the 2008 campaign.

"Two ex-wives is one ex-wife too many for most evangelicals,"[25] Land said about Newt Gingrich during the 2012 campaign.

Land's now changed his tune to help Trump win in 2016. Are we allowing politicians to redefine our positions on marriage? Sad! Jerry Falwell, Jr., who also joined Trump's evangelical advisory board, used a marriage metaphor to justify his support for Trump. When explaining why he supports Trump despite some differences, Falwell retorted, "How many of you can honestly say that you even agree with your spouse on everything?"[26] Is that how we see Trump? As a spouse? Considering how faithful Trump's been to his first two wives, why would Falwell expect different treatment (after all, Falwell's not nearly as good looking)?

Sadly, this marriage between churches and a political party hasn't been good for the churches. By marrying ourselves off to one party, we silenced our prophetic independence and made ourselves dependent on another kingdom. We've wrapped our legs together to the point we can't even figure out which is ours and which belongs to a political party. Is this the behavior of people who preach character matters and claim to trust in God's commands and provision? Before we wake up in the morning and look over with regret at who we're cuddling with, we need to keep a prophetic distance from candidates.

Cuban Baptists singing praises to God during a Sunday service in 2016.

"Oh Son of God, Receive today all glory, The honor and the praise."

Chapter 5: I Pledge Allegiance

Following the 2015 Supreme Court decision in *Obergefell v. Hodges* that legalized same-sex marriage in the U.S., some critics of the decision started a flag protest. Rit Varriale, senior pastor at Elizabeth Baptist Church in Shelby, North Carolina, changed the order of the flags on his church's flagpole. Rather than the traditional order of the U.S. flag on top and the Christian flag second, he put the Christian flag on top. Such an ordering violates the U.S. Flag Code that requires the U.S. flag to fly higher than any other. Yet, Varriale, an Army veteran who graduated from The Citadel, now believes the U.S. flag should fly second.

"If you stop and think about it, [flag etiquette] is inconsistent with what the Bible teaches us," Varriale said. "We are first and foremost Christians who are called to serve the living God."[1]

"Before our accountability to government is our accountability to God," he added. "So from a Christian perspective, our flag etiquette is completely improper. We should be flying the Christian flag above the American flag."[2]

Varriale found inspiration for the effort after seeing an African-American Baptist church flying the flags that way and then talking with the pastor. Interestingly, Varriale's church didn't even actually have flags before this protest. They built a flagpole just in time for the Sunday closest to the Fourth of July in 2015 and then on that day put the Christian flag up over the U.S. flag. I don't agree with all of Varriale's thoughts on church-state relations, but he makes a fascinating point with his prophetic flip of the flags. What he's noting is that we cannot truly divorce religion and politics. I don't think we should mix church and state like he often proposes at government buildings and in public schools, but I also think we must not mix the ice cream and manure at our churches (try not to think of that image at the next church potluck). The movement to fly the Christian flag above the U.S. flag spread to some other churches, but remains a minority perspective. Stan Welch, pastor of West Asheville Baptist Church in Asheville, North Carolina, explained why they joined the effort.

"We're not protesting; we're proclaiming," he explained. "If someone thinks their first allegiance is to their country first and not God, that's against the Bible."[3]

Perhaps not surprisingly, several of the news stories published about churches taking this stand include criticism from people in the local communities. The churches are accused of disrespecting our country, our military, and more. They're called "un-American" and critics urge they be arrested (it turns out, though, the U.S. Flag Code includes no provisions for enforcement or penalties). The responses show how deep people's allegiances can run to their country. Making a theological statement that the Kingdom of God demands our primary allegiance is a religious statement. But it's also clearly a political statement. As the criticism shows, many people—including many people in our churches—reject the religious-political implications. Many people shout "amen" when they hear "America First" (a slogan popularized by American anti-Semitics in the 1940s and reused by Donald Trump to describe his foreign policy). But for Kingdom people seeking to remain faithful, we must declare, "Kingdom First."

We cannot really serve both our divine Kingdom and our national kingdom. Jesus warned us we can't serve two masters. As he suggests, we can only fully serve one. They are not separate but equal. One always trumps the other. We can only pledge true allegiance to one. The word "allegiance" conjures an era we in the U.S. generally don't understand. The word came to English from the Anglo-French term *legaunce*, which described the loyalty a vassal/servant owed to his lord (or liege). When you pledge allegiance, you are submitting to a master or lord. You're saying that lord—be it a person, a god, a nation, an ideology, or whatever—gets to decide what you believe and how you live. If a political party is your lord, you'll support their nominee no matter what. If Jesus is your Lord, it means you'll say no to other would-be lords. That's where martyrs come into our faith history. They're the ones who submitted to their Lord when asked by another "lord" to follow.

In mid-June I drove by a Baptist church whose sign caught my eye. It declared, "Patriotic Service 7-3." Behind the sign, the church placed flags on three poles in this order of prioritization: U.S., Missouri, Christian. I found the sign interesting as it suggested they had nothing more important to promote for the rest of June. Then it struck me. Every Sunday is a patriotic service! Each Sunday we come together to sing our patriotic hymns about the Kingdom to which we are to give first allegiance. Each Sunday we come together to hear a patriotic speech (sermon). And some churches even go through a patriotic ritual each Sunday as they demonstrate their allegiance to the Kingdom by taking the bread and cup. If on any given Sunday we're not having a patriotic service for the Kingdom, we're doing something wrong.

When Republican 2008 presidential nominee John McCain used "Country First" as his campaign slogan, it created a couple of interesting moments at the Republican convention. During the second evening, Christian musician Rachel Lampa performed. As she sang, people waved signs declaring "Country First." Meanwhile the massive wall of TV screens behind her featured a waving American flag with each red or white bar nearly as tall as her. It created an interesting mix of messages. For instance, she sang "When I Fall," which is to God even though it never names God.

"And I know I'm not forsaken, and I'll never be alone," she sang. "When I fall, when I fall, you will still be standing."

Those not familiar with Lampa as a Christian musician could easily be lulled into thinking she's singing about the United States—especially with that large flag and those "Country First" signs. Similarly, she then sang "Blessed" where she declared "I am blessed, I am blessed." Although the song does reference "Oh, Lord," the overall presentation seemed like a patriotic ode to nationalistic blessings. Perhaps feeling the tension between the two kingdoms, John McCain's pastor included an interesting line in his prayer that concluded the convention two nights later. Just moments after McCain's acceptance speech and with confetti and balloons still floating around, Dan Yeary, pastor of North Phoenix Baptist Church, approached the microphone.

"O, Lord, in humility we ask that you remind us that we cannot put our 'country first' unless you are foremost," Yeary declared toward the end of his prayer. "For as Jesus taught his disciples, 'thine is the Kingdom and the power and the glory forever.' Amen."[4]

Yeary's comment still strikes me as interesting. After all, 'foremost' is just a fancy way of saying 'first.' You cannot have one thing 'first' and another thing 'foremost.' It's like how you cannot serve two masters. Yet, even though awkward, he still attempted to offer a prophetic word that we as Christians are not, in fact, called to put 'country first.' We are citizens of another Kingdom—and that King does deserve all power and glory. Yeary's prayer helps highlight a tension that exists in the realms of religion and politics.

Each Sunday we find politics in our churches—we just might not notice it. Flags are just one symbol of that struggle for ultimate allegiance. When we fly the U.S. flag above the Christian flag, we're saying something religious and something political. When we put the U.S. flag in our sanctuary even while we recite how God loves the whole world, we're saying something religious and something political. When we sing hymns about the King of kings and the Lord of lords, we're saying something religious and something political. This means even the core declaration of our faith—to follow Jesus as Lord—carries inherent political implications. So before we can accept the politics of Hillary Clinton or Donald Trump (or any other politician), we must first understand the politics of Jesus. Before we can really evaluate the politics of the Republican or Democratic parties, we must first know the politics of the Kingdom. My concern in 2016 is less about what Trump and Clinton are doing and saying and more about what Jesus is doing and saying. So in this chapter we'll think carefully about the politics embedded in our religious faith and worship. Many of the ideas in this chapter come from my third book.[5] The subtitle of the book explains the focus: *religious worship as political action*.

Christ is Lord

Religious worship is political. To say "Christ is Lord" is to say Caesar is not. It's to say President Barack Obama is not. It's to say President Hillary Clinton or President Donald Trump will not be. The Roman empire didn't crucify Jesus because of heresy. They crucified him as a threat to their political sovereignty and rule. Thus, the biblical narrative depicts Jesus crucified as a political insurrectionist with a political charge hanging above him on the cross: "This is the King of the Jews." The religious and political cannot be separated. To reject the politics of Jesus would be to reject the spiritual teachings of Jesus. The question is not if we will bring politics into religion, but what politics?

Religious worship inherently carries political messages, expectations, and deeds. After all, the word "liturgy" comes from the Greek word *leitourgia*, a political term describing service given for the city-state or political community. Aristotle used the word with this political connotation in his book *Politics* as he explained how to best organize a political community. When we worship, we pledge allegiance to our political community. The question, then, is who will we worship? To whom will we pledge allegiance? We've often spiritualized ideas like "Christ is Lord." We act like he's just Lord of our hearts. We almost act like he's just some little Jiminy Cricket giving us moral advice. Or that he'll rule in Heaven in the age to come, but not here and now. But to say "Jesus is Lord" during the age of Caesar could get a Christian killed on a cross—as a lot of them discovered.

The liturgy that Christians join together to perform sits at the heart of religious worship and forms the basis for understanding a church's ecclesiastical practices. Terms like "ecclesiastical" (relating to a church or its clergy) and "ecclesiology" (the study of a church's theology or architecture) come from the Greek word *ekklesia*, which originally meant a political assembly of the citizens of a city-state. This Greek word appears over 100 times in the New Testament to describe the meeting of Christians. That means early Christian writers borrowed a political term to describe their worship services as an assembly of a kingdom's citizens. This is not an accident. Many words existed that the biblical writers could've employed to describe the church. They could've used a religious gathering term (like synagogue) or a family relational term or a host of other options. But they chose a political word to describe their gatherings.

In the U.S. we often seem to lose the understanding of the political consequences of worship, but in other countries they get it. During a trip to Turkey a few years ago, I met pastors there (and pastors from other nations like Syria and Iraq) who understand how the act of going to church can be viewed as a political threat. Such an act could bring violence, police harassment, or other types of persecution. Later I saw this same understanding of worship as a potent political act from pastors during two trips to Cuba. Governments around the world persecute Christians. They don't do it merely for religious disagreements. These are also deeply political decisions as political governments take political actions against members who give first priority to another *ekklesia*. Perhaps in the U.S. we've too spiritualized the teachings of Jesus and the prophets. We are called to follow our Lord and submit to his Kingdom here and now. Jesus doesn't seek to serve only as Lord of our soul. He doesn't desire to rule only as King of our Sunday mornings. A true Lord and King holds authority over all aspects of his subjects' lives.

"God's reign has profound political consequences," explained Erwin Stutzman, executive director of the Mennonite Church USA. "The faithful church, not any political party, best serves as example and herald of God's reign in the world. The church is called to be an expression of God's reign, a community of the kingdom of God on earth."[6]

This doesn't mean we shouldn't engage in presidential campaigns and other political processes, but it should transform how we engage in politics. Perhaps the most potent expression of this Kingdom citizenship comes as we gather together to celebrate communion. Each time we take the bread and the cup, we reaffirm our first allegiance to our King and his Kingdom. Ben Irwin, an Episcopalian author wrote about the power of communion during the 2012 presidential election. He noted the political implications of communion that we too often overlook.

"We already have a king," he argued. "There is no 'red state vs. blue state' in the kingdom of God. We are one body. We eat the same bread, drink of the same cup, serve the same Lord. No president or party can claim our highest allegiance or compete for our first love. We are already spoken for."[7]

Amen! Communion is a deeply political act. One of the most powerful moments of communion for me came last year during the Baptist World Congress in Durban, South Africa. Thousands of Baptists from more than 80 nations shared together in that sacred moment. With this profound act, we said we are one. We will not allow difference to divide us. We will not allow artificial national boundaries to divide us. We will not allow walls to divide us. By pledging allegiance first to the Kingdom, we aligned ourselves across borders with each other. That is an act of commitment with serious political implications if we truly live it out!

In fact, that type of religious politics frightened key thinkers who helped lay the foundation for the modern nation-state. Fearing a church that transcends national boundaries would undermine the sovereignty and power of a country, philosophers like Thomas Hobbes and Jean-Jacques Rousseau tried to create ways to remove religion from the political realm by privatizing religion. Their theories on modern states, religion, and the public square largely impacted our own society. William Cavanaugh, a brilliant political theologian, explains and critiques the philosophy of Rousseau and others. While Cavanaugh disagrees with the priorities of modern state philosophers, he acknowledges they correctly recognized the political potential of communion and a globally-connected church.

"The new state required unchallenged authority within its borders, and so the domestication of the Church," Cavanaugh explains. "Church leaders became acolytes of the state as the religion of the state replaced that of the Church, or more accurately, the very concept of religion as separable from the Church was invented."[8]

"The Eucharist transgresses national boundaries and redefines who our fellow-citizens are," Cavanaugh added. "Rousseau was right to note that communion among churches is a threat to the unity of the state."[9]

As I've written elsewhere,[10] perhaps the most potent example of this can be found on the U.S.-Mexico border. A couple of Methodist pastors hold Sunday services on the border, giving communion to those on both sides of the wall. Meeting at "Friendship Park" in San Diego (United States) and Tijuana (Mexico), they call their services "El Faro:

The Border Church / La Iglesia Fronteriza." It's a prophetic witness that declares the Kingdom of God doesn't stop at borders and walls.

"[E]very Sunday afternoon people from both nations will gather to share communion, a reminder that neither God nor God's people will be limited by national boundaries," they explain on their Facebook page. "By bringing people together from both nations and sharing the sacrament of communion across the international boundary, we witness to the truth that God's grace and love does not distinguish between persons of different nationalities, and we stand in solidarity—both practically and symbolically—with people who are separated from their loved ones by virtue of their immigration status."[11]

This type of service would alarm Rousseau—and I suspect it terrifies and angers Donald Trump as well! But this is our calling. Christians around the world are united as fellow members of the same Body. When they suffer, we are to suffer. When they are honored, we are to rejoice. What God has put together, let not man (politician or otherwise) put asunder.[12] Our first allegiance must be to the Kingdom, not to any nation or especially to any political party.

After years of many religious and political leaders attempting to unite Christianity with a political party, we need to declare our independence. In the midst of yet another bitter election that pits

Christians against one another, we need to reassert our unity in Christ. After all, our leader was coronated, not inaugurated! It does not matter who is president, Christ is King! It does not matter who is in the Oval Office, Christ is still on the Throne! As I noted in a sermon nine days before the 2012 election, "it doesn't matter if Barack O'Caesar or Mitt Caesarney wins, God will still be on the throne." Christians in the U.S. must quit looking for salvation and hope in the ballot box or Washington, D.C. We must offer an independent moral witness instead of becoming part of the partisan political games. Churches in the United States are still too partisan and polarized. Too often Christians are leading the way in slinging mud in campaigns. Too often we add to the polarization and the division. Too often we are tempted by the siren calls of power. Too often we give to Caesar what is God's.

"Every king had a prophet, a critic on the margins, a little thorn in their side," Shane Claibrone and Chris Haw reminded us in the brilliant book *Jesus for President*. "While we are taught history mostly through the lives of kings and presidents, God tells history through the lives of the prophets."[13]

The body of Christ is being torn apart by partisan politics and ungodly quests for power. We need the church to be the church. We need a public witness that our faith and hope remains in God, not

Washington. We need to come together to declare "Christ is King!" and "Christ is Lord!" No matter what happens in Washington or elsewhere, Christ is King! No matter who rules our nation or other nations, Christ is Lord! He was not elected by the people and inaugurated; he was coronated. Politicians tried to kill him, but his reign has no term limits. Christ is Risen! Christ is King! Christ is Lord! Amen!

Seeking Sanctuary

During the last couple of days of the 2016 campaign in Iowa before Hawkeye State voters went to their caucus sites, I trekked up to catch some of the action and report for *Ethics Daily*. I attended a Republican caucus and rallies for Jeb! Bush, Marco Rubio, Ted Cruz, Rand Paul, Trump, and Bernie Sanders. Several of the candidates wove religious rhetoric into their stump speeches. None, however, compared to that of Cruz. The rally I attended with him (and Glenn Beck) occurred in a church's sanctuary on Sunday night. As I neared the church, I realized Cruz pulled in a better crowd than the average Sunday as cars overflowed out of the parking lot onto the grass around the church and down the street for several blocks. Apparently political revivals are popular! As I walked toward the church, greeters welcomed me—as did several Cruz signs taped up on the outside of the church building. Inside, other Cruz signs tacked on the walls hung out with signs about Jesus and salvation. Communion plates had been stacked in the back of the room, pushed out of the way. Small kids played with toys at the base of the plates as their parents stood on tiptoes, straining to see the speakers.

The screens normally used to project praise song lyrics and sermon notes instead glowed with Cruz videos and logos. Beck warmed up the crowd by cursing as he praised the glory of American might. When he said Hillary Clinton shouldn't be in the White House but in jail, someone in the political congregation yelled, "Preach, brother, preach." Cruz took the stage, making a grand entrance down the aisle as people reached out to touch him as he passed by them. Like a fiery revival preacher, he stirred up the crowd with his sound-bite stump speech. He called America the "shining city on a hill." People clapped and cheered. I wondered if there was a Bible in the house to double-check that claim (hint: check Matthew 5 to find which Kingdom that phrase describes). With a cross just off to the side of him, he preached against immigrants and for bombing people. I somehow managed to leave without pulling out a whip and turning over tables!

What upset me most was the location. If we know that religious worship is inherently political, then we must be careful not to push aside that politics for an alternative message. It's one thing for a politician to be anti-immigrant and refugee. It's another thing for a church. After all, the political message of the Bible remains quite clear on that issue.

"When immigrants live in your land with you, you must not cheat them," we hear God say in Leviticus. "Any immigrant who lives with you must be treated as if they were one of your citizens. You must love them as yourself, because you were immigrants in the land of Egypt; I am the Lord your God."[14]

"[God] enacts justice for orphans and widows, and he loves immigrants, giving them food and clothing," we learn in Deuteronomy. "That means you must also love immigrants because you were immigrants in Egypt."[15] Deuteronomy 10:18-19

"The Lord: who protects immigrants, who helps orphans and widows, but who makes the way of the wicked twist and turn!"[16] a psalmist declared.

I could keep going for multiple pages. If we're going to talk about immigrants and refugees in our churches, we should hear a pastor preaching love instead of a politician preaching fear. Cruz, the son of an immigrant-turned-preacher, should particularly know better and catch the reminders to the Hebrew people to love immigrants because they were once immigrants. As we saw in the previous chapter, politicians holding campaign rallies in churches is, unfortunately, not something unique to Cruz. In fact, most of the candidates this year (in both parties) did so. Both Clinton and Trump ended up in churches and religious gatherings during the primaries, and both will continue that approach during the general election.

For the church to be the church during the 2016 presidential campaign (and beyond), perhaps the first step is to quit letting candidates into the pulpit! Conservative Christian groups should stop inviting Republicans and liberal Christian groups should stop inviting Democrats. Fortunately, some pastors are pushing this approach. Republican presidential hopeful Ben Carson received an invite to speak at the 2015 Southern Baptist Convention (SBC)'s Pastor's Conference, a two-day event packed with preaching just before the SBC's annual business meeting. Some conservative Southern Baptist pastors quickly protested the invitation.

"There continue to be perceptions in our culture that the SBC is in bed with the Republican Party, and actions such as having Dr. Carson speak at the SBC Pastor's Conference only prove that perception correct," a group of pastors wrote. "These perceptions continue to hamper our witness in an increasingly purple America, where missional efforts are often misunderstood as Southern Baptists asking people to become more politically conservative. .... In fact, we have more in common with a born again Christian who is a registered Democrat, than we do with a universalist Seventh-Day Adventist who is a conservative."[17]

"We are concerned because in our evangelical climate it is often easy to confuse what it means to be a follower of Christ with what it means to be a patriotic American," the pastors added."[18]

After that statement and others sparked controversy in religious and mainstream media, Carson and the SBC leaders pulled the plug on him speaking at the event. Thomas Kidd, professor of history at Baylor University (a Southern Baptist school) and the author of multiple books on religious history, argued the SBC-Carson incident showed evangelicals need to stop inviting political candidates to speak at religious gatherings.

"By highlighting the political insiders of the week at Kingdom-oriented events, we keep giving the watching world the impression that the Gospel of Jesus Christ is inextricably connected to voting Republican," Kidd explained. "And that our talk about Jesus, grace, and forgiveness is really just pious window-dressing for a core political agenda. Annual denominational meetings for pastors should attend to issues such as the best preaching practices, evangelism, missions, reaching and discipling young people, praying for revival, etc.—isn't that enough to do without giving keynote space to random presidential candidates?"[19]

We should remember that when a politician is running for office, each speaking event is carefully considered. Will it help them win some votes? If so, they'll go for the opportunity. If an event might upset more people than it excites or if it involves a lot of time and money for few potential votes, they'll decline. That's not cynical; that's just practical and smart if someone actually wants to win. So if a candidate wants to speak in your church or at your religious event, it means they think it'll help them win the election. That alone should give us pause. Do we want to turn over our Kingdom event for someone to win an office in another kingdom? Even the best candidate—one who we proudly support in public and vote for in private—hardly seems worth the tradeoff. The 2016 campaign seems like the perfect year to announce our independence from political parties and declare our allegiance to the politics of the Kingdom.

Saw this "Christ is Risen!" sign near primary election day in 2016.

Now there's a campaign sign I can support!

Chapter 6: What Shall We Do?

As the 2016 election drags on, it sadly seems nearly each day some Christian pastor or leader decides to publicly let party trump principles. One endorsement I found particularly upsetting came as evangelist and author Anne Graham Lotz did so quite quickly after Trump wrapped up the nomination. I've thought highly of Lotz for some time before this.

"I said that whoever was the Republican presidential nominee I would vote for, and it looks like it may be Donald Trump," Lotz said after the other candidates dropped out. "So I would find it difficult to vote for a Democrat at this point because of the platforms so I will vote for whoever the Republican nominee is."[1]

I still find Lotz's explanation quite stunning. Her litmus test for who to vote for boils down to nothing other than party identification. That's essentially saying, "I'm a Republican first." That's the definition of letting party trump principles. Having decided to follow the GOP, no turning back, Lotz then sought to justify her decision with scripture. That, by the way, is the opposite direction we should work. If we pick up the Bible to find a passage after we've made a decision, we're using the Bible as a magical trump card and not our moral guidebook. For a proof-text, Lotz turned to the book of Daniel (which just happens to be the subject of her newest book).

"Daniel was a man who lived under four world emperors—none of whom were children of Abraham, none of whom were members of God's family—but God used all of them … all four ended up giving praise to the God of Daniel because of what they saw in Daniel's life," Lotz argued. "The first one was Nebuchadnezzar, and God actually refers to Nebuchadnezzar as 'my servant' in the Old Testament."[2]

"So my feeling is whoever is the Republican nominee, whoever gets into the Oval Office, and if it's a Democrat or a Republican, whoever is in that position of power, I feel like we need to pray for that person because Nebuchadnezzar was somebody who was wicked, he was evil," she added. "God used him in an incredible way, but in the end, Nebuchadnezzar gave glory to the God of Daniel, and his life was changed."[3]

The basic point Lotz offers is correct: as Christians we must be faithful regardless of who sits in the Oval Office, just as Daniel remained faithful regardless who sat on the throne. But there's a huge leap from that perspective to endorsing Trump. Daniel did absolutely nothing to put Nebuchadnezzar (or the others) on the throne. Daniel didn't endorse him. Comparing Trump to Nebuchadnezzar is quite interesting because, as Lotz said, Nebuchadnezzar was "wicked" and "evil." If she sees Trump like Nebuchadnezzar, are we really to endorse him? Let's briefly recall how Daniel and his friends actually responded to Nebuchadnezzar and the other rulers.

Under Nebuchadnezzar's rule, Daniel and others were kidnapped and forced into slavery (so I'm going to say Daniel probably wouldn't vote for Nebuchadnezzar). Nebuchadnezzar also destroyed the temple in Jerusalem. The first thing Daniel did in the text is refuse to partake of the royal food and wine. It's quite risky for a slave to demand different food. Today it seems we, too, need God's wisdom to reject what Trump's trying to feed us. Later, we find Nebuchadnezzar's ego getting the best of him. He built a big golden image. I'm sure it was classy, just the best. Maybe it even said "Nebuchadnezzar" in big golden letters. Three of Daniel's cohort refused to bow (and we should assume Daniel would've as well, but must've been elsewhere at the moment). Nebuchadnezzar burned with anger and ordered the three—Hananiah, Mishael, and Azariah (also known as Shadrach, Meshach, and Abednego)—thrown into a fiery furnace. He might've even first urged people to "punch them in the face" and "rough them up" before getting the crowd to start chanting "Babylon, Babylon" as the security guards dragged the three men toward the furnace. Even then, the three refused to bow as they remained true to their conscience and their real King.

Daniel returns to the story with a message for Nebuchadnezzar—and it's not an endorsement. Daniel predicted Nebuchadnezzar will be driven out of office because of his sins and wander around insane like an animal. It's the type of message that could anger an unstable man enough to cause him to throw you into a furnace. Yet, Daniel prophetically delivered the message anyway—and it came to pass. Daniel repeated this with the next king—Belshazzar—and once again his prophetic word of condemnation is fulfilled. Even as Daniel predicted the end of the reign of two kings, he did nothing to endorse a new king or help them rise to power. He just kept following God, as the next story demonstrates. During the reign of King Darius, Daniel famously ended up in a den of lions. Why? Well, it's clearly not for endorsing Darius. Rather, Daniel remained faithful to his real King and refused to allow a leader's rules to trump principles.

All of that is to say Lotz only got it half right. We are to remain faithful like Daniel and the other three. But that doesn't mean we must endorse or align ourselves with a party. We must be willing to reject the royal wine, the golden idol, and the unjust law—whatever the consequences. If Lotz is correct that Trump is like Nebuchadnezzar (and it's actually a decent analogy), then she unfortunately finds herself as someone other than Daniel, Shadrach, Meshach, or Abednego. King Nebuchadnezzar ... uh, excuse me ... President Trump remains unlikely to take punitive actions against those who endorse him. He'll instead focus his egotistical wrath against those who refused to bow as they prophetically challenged him. If we wish to be Daniel, we must reject the approach of Lotz and refuse to allow party to trump principles. Besides Nebuchadnezzar, perhaps we could see Trump playing the part of King Xerxes, who tossed aside one wife (Queen Vashti) when she refused to show off her body at his party. He then held an international beauty contest to find a new wife. Or worse, Trump provides echoes of King Herod, who so burned with lust for his stepdaughter/niece that he chopped off John the baptizer's head. Neither are good examples of someone we should endorse. Rather, God's people in place for times such as those prophetically challenged the evil plans of those kings.

Somehow we must learn to resist the temptation of power. Michael Gerson, conservative *Washington Post* columnist and former chief speechwriter for George W. Bush, lambasted evangelicals endorsing Trump for falling for a temptation akin to "the third temptation of Christ"[4] of seeking to use the government to fulfill the work of the Kingdom. That temptation was a simple one as the devil showed Jesus "all the kingdoms of the world" and said, "All this I will give you if you will bow down and worship me."[5] It's the test the four Hebrew heroes in the book of Daniel faced. They could advance up in royal power by bowing to the king or his idol. We face the same temptation: let's take control of this kingdom!

"The emperor, or king, or president offers to further the mission of the church," Gerson explained about this temptation. "The church, in turn, provides legitimacy to power."[6]

Gerson noted there could be a pragmatic argument for backing Trump as Trump might—he stressed it's unclear since Trump can't be trusted—give the nation a conservative Supreme Court justice. But Gerson also noted what's lost in the trade-off is much worse. Once again, it's the ice cream—not the manure—that stands to lose. Gerson argued it's "a massive, disorienting shift" for "evangelicals to endorse a political figure who has engaged in creepy sex talk on the radio, boasted about his extramarital affairs, made a fortune from gambling and bragged about his endowment on national television."[7] Gerson added that deciding to "bear the mark of Trump"[8] also means supporting a candidate who urges religious discrimination, inflames racial tensions, advocates war crime, promotes undemocratic values, and sparks fear of refugees and other powerless peoples.

"Evangelical Christians are not merely choosing a certain political outcome," he added. "They are determining their public character—the way they are viewed by others and, ultimately, the way they view themselves. ... In legitimizing the presumptive Republican nominee, evangelicals are not merely accepting who he is; they are changing who they are."[9]

"To everything there is a season," Gerson added. "This is the time for principled dissent."[10]

Gerson's right. By standing strong like Daniel, Gerson will keep his prophetic witness intact after November. We must do so as well. If we want to offer a faithful, prophetic witness to our new president in 2017 and beyond, we need to be careful how we act in 2016. We will now turn to that topic as we consider how the church can be the church during the 2016 presidential campaign. I'll offer five actions we can take.

VOTE YOUR CONSCIENCE

1. Vote Your Conscience

On November 8, go vote. When you do, vote your conscience. Please ignore the voices—including the Christian ones—trying to justify support for a thrice-married casino mogul known for vulgarity, violence, bigotry, and racism. We must not align ourselves with evil policies and rhetoric. Our Christian witness is more important than the electoral hopes of the Republican Party. Our Kingdom is more important than the Democratic Party. Some people will argue that if you don't vote for Trump that's essentially the same as voting for Clinton. When you don't vote for Trump, Clinton's vote total doesn't go up by one. She'll still have to earn more votes than him. Similarly, not voting for Clinton isn't a vote for Trump. The idea that if you're not voting for one candidate you're voting for the other is only true if you've given full and complete allegiance to a party. If we're owned by the GOP, then not voting for Trump hurts our masters. If we're owned by Democrats, not voting for Clinton hurts our masters. But if we're voting principles, we're allowed to reject any party—and they are responsible for that loss for nominating someone unfit for office. If a member of a baseball squad doesn't show up it could help the other team win. But we're not called to be Republicans or Democrats first. Our real team is the Kingdom of God.

Don't forgot there will be numerous other important races on the ballot, some of which (like U.S. congressional members) may serve as a check on whoever wins the White House. There are many races in which you can positively advocate for values you hold dear and policies you support. The presidential race gets the most attention, but local races have a large impact—and sometimes a larger impact—on our daily lives. Read about the candidates, go meet them at events and ask them questions, press the candidates on issues you find important, and then vote. And stay involved after the election process, following up with the winners and urging them to implement moral and just policies.

If you don't live in one of the few swing states that will decide the election, this year is a great chance to show displeasure in our broken primary process that gave us the two least popular nominees in modern presidential politics. As of the start of August, the swing states likely to decide the election are Florida, Pennsylvania, Ohio, North Carolina, Michigan, Colorado, Iowa, New Hampshire, and Nevada. By election day, the list of states that will decide the election will likely shrink. For those of us living in most states that won't swing the election, we can protest both Trump and Clinton by voting for a third-party candidate. That's what I'll do on November 8 since Missouri is unlikely to matter. If you stay home, your protest is hardly noticed. Voter turnout is already really low and it doesn't seem to shame politicians, so why would you sitting on a couch bother them? And don't write-in a name unless you've checked your state laws to make sure it'll count. Some states don't allow write-in votes, and in most states a write-in candidate needs to file some paperwork. What that means is if you write in a candidate, some states won't count it. It'll be as if you stayed home on your couch.

So if you want to make sure the candidates don't dismiss you as lazy or indifferent—as they will if you don't bother to vote—then vote for a third-party option on the ballot. In most modern presidential elections, all third-party candidates combined receive less than two percent of the presidential votes. In only three elections over the last 40 years has that third-party amount topped four percent and the most recent occurred 20 years ago with Ross Perot's second run. So if the total third-party vote soars this year, it'll be a more noticeable protest than staying home. If total third-party votes top ten percent, it'll tell both major parties that many Americans took the time to vote just to say 'no' to both of them. If Trump and/or Clinton falls below 40 percent, it'll be a huge collapse that would send a strong message to their party. But if as white evangelicals we hold our nose (apparently squeezing until it bleeds) and vote for Trump, it'll tell the Republican Party they don't need to listen to Christians to still get our votes. I fear the exit polls on election night will show white evangelicals going strong for Trump. As of late July, more than three-quarters of white evangelicals were saying they would vote for Trump, which is about what all other recent Republican presidential candidates received. If Trump doesn't underperform an average Republican nominee, then we're allowing party to trump principles. If that high percentage of support holds on November 8, our gospel witness will take yet another huge hit this year.

The two alternative parties that'll do the best—and the only two expected to be on more than 40 state ballots—are the Libertarian Party (www.lp.org) and the Green Party (www.gp.org). Check them out and figure out which candidate you like more. You may not find one you like that much, but voting for either sends a strong message to the two major parties, which might be the most powerful thing we can say on the ballot this year. If you still can't bring yourself to support one of the third-party candidates, just write in my name (Brian Kaylor) and hopefully it'll count! Let's send a message with our votes.

2. Gently Rebuke

One thing I've done in this book is name names of many Christian pastors and leaders who've publicly made endorsements putting party head of principles. Some have done so while expressing regret. Others have gone full-throated in their defenses, even rhetorically baptizing Trump as some sort of new believer. My naming of names is intentional. We need to hold our leaders accountable. Some of those I've named I used to respect. For prominent Christian leaders to use their media platforms to tie our churches to one of these candidates remains highly problematic as we face the two least popular nominees in modern presidential elections.

Just as Jeremiah and other prophets called out those who wrongly courted evil, powerful kings, we must demand our leaders today to repent if they allow party to trump principles. Within our own circle of influence, we can all do this. If you know a pastor or church leader making public endorsements, urge them to stop. Each one of us is called to be an ambassador for Christ, as Paul wrote in 'Two' Corinthians 5:20. That's interesting language. Like an ambassador for the U.S. who lives in another country but represents the U.S., we are ambassadors for the Kingdom and just happen to live in U.S. right now.

Thus, each of us should feel called to represent our King in our churches, our neighborhoods, and the public square.

There's a delicate dance many pastors and Christian leaders try out each four years. It's not the tango—and they're usually not that good at it. It's the I'm-not-endorsing-a-candidate-even-as-I-wink-at-my-preference dance. This election particularly makes such doublespeak problematic. If someone urges support for Clinton or Trump, then they've endorsed a candidate even if they don't use the word "endorse." We must hold Christian leaders accountable for their public support of Trump. For instance, when Richard Land of Southern Evangelical Seminary (who used the marriage and consummation metaphor in 1998 that I discussed in chapter three) joined Trump's evangelical advisory board designed to help Trump win, Land insisted, "I have not endorsed Donald Trump." By that declaration, Land must only mean he has not yet used the 'e'-word. Land previously announced he will "vote against Hillary Clinton and I don't believe in third party candidates." He added that Christians must "help the lesser evil prevail over the greater evil," adding that "Clinton is the greater evil." He clearly said he's voting for Trump and thinks all Christians have a moral obligation to do so as well. That's an endorsement! To suggest otherwise is dishonest. We must let our 'yes' be 'yes' and our 'no' be 'no.'

3. Craft Alternative Messages

Like many states this year, Missouri held its presidential primary during Lent as Christians spiritually prepared for Easter. Missouri voted the Tuesday before 'holy week' and some states even voted during 'holy week.' A few days before voting, I noticed a sign in my neighborhood as I walked our dog one morning. The same size as the political signs that also appeared in a few places in the neighborhood, the purple-and-white sign declared "Christ is Risen!" Now there's a political sign I can support. It went down after Easter, but it got me thinking about the need for alternative religious-political messages during this nasty campaign year. We can join the culture in shouting for Clinton or Trump or we can hide quietly until it's all over. Or we can do something better and point a different way. Old Testament scholar Walter Brueggemann argues that we need more "prophetic imagination" in churches today. He calls the prophets poets and artists trying to shake up the people by saying the unsayable, thinking the unthinkable, imagining the unimaginable. The 2016 presidential campaign calls for such responses. Rather than quietly hide, we must speak out with much-needed political messages.

Perhaps we need to make our own campaign yard signs. Slogans could include "Christ is King," "We Already Have a Savior," "Kingdom First," "The Real Commander-in-Chief Isn't Up for Election," "Light Trumps Darkness," or "Faith Trumps Fear" (or maybe even "Vote Your Conscience"). If Trump or Clinton shows up for a campaign visit in your area, go and stand outside with a sign. You could have one protesting the candidates on specific issues (like Eric Teetsel did when 1,000 evangelical pastors met with Trump). Or you could go with an alternative religious-political message to remind people this isn't our primary Kingdom. As former New York City Mayor Rudy Giuliani angrily offered false attacks on refugees during his speech on the first night of the Republican National Convention in July, someone in the arena unfurled a large banner that read "Refugees Welcome." It's unfortunate such a prophetic rebuke was necessary, but I'm thankful someone offered that message. Another protestor unfurled a banner two nights later during Trump's acceptance speech. That banner prophetically declared, "Build Bridges Not Walls."

Some people protest Trump with a Mexican flag, which is kind of funny. Somebody in Scotland did this by flying a Mexican flag next to Trump's golf course there just before a Trump speech there. That's quite a global message. That would be interesting to see at a church when Trump comes to town. Maybe it could be done in conjunction with a special prayer service for immigrants and refugees. Or maybe we could fly an Iraqi flag since both candidates supported George W. Bush's decision to invade—an act that destabilized the region and has led to the ancient Christian community in that nation nearly being completely destroyed. We are part of a Kingdom that transcends national boundaries (as discussed in the previous chapter). Thus, we are united with our fellow citizens who happen to live in Mexico, Syria, Libya, Iraq, China, or anywhere else.

As you think of ways to bring some much-needed prophetic imagination into this campaign season, post them on Instagram and tag me (@BrianKaylor). I'll post some on a page on my website throughout the campaign: www.BrianKaylor.com/p/2016.html. Let's conspire together on how the church can offer a prophetic voice in a time desperately in need of prophets.

4. Study the Bible (and the News)

Karl Barth, one of the most influential theologians of the 20th Century, noted the importance of reading both the Bible and newspapers—and making sure we use the correct one to interpret the other. He urged his students "to take your Bible and take your newspaper, and read both. But interpret newspapers from your Bible."[11]

Barth clearly did this as he raised his voice against Adolf Hitler and Nazism as early as 1934 (and lost his professorship in Germany for it). The call of Christians in each age is to similarly read both the Bible and the news and let the Bible serve as the interpretive standard. To read the Bible without paying attention to the world around us is to mute our prophetic voice. To read the newspapers first and then find biblical proof-texts is to transform ourselves into court prophets.

During a campaign, it can be tempting to allow candidates and pundits to set the agenda of what we talk about and what we think. They want us to divide, act on fear, and accept their soundbite half-truths. People of the Book must offer a different path. We must use our prophetic voices to preach the politics of the Kingdom. I'm not calling on pastors to endorse candidates—directly or even subtly—from the pulpit. That's allowing the politics of another kingdom to take precedence. But we need our pastors to preach the Bible with an eye on the news. If we preach only about the afterlife and ignore the current issues facing our communities, nation, and world, then we've made the gospel irrelevant. When politicians demonize refugees and stir us up to fear and hate refugees, pastors need to proclaim what the scriptures teach us about loving and welcoming the refugees. As the political rhetoric against refugees heated up last fall, that's exactly what several

Christian organizations (including the National Association of Evangelicals, World Relief, and World Vision) did by urging churches to recognize "National Refugee Sunday" on December 13. They held a 2016 version at the end of June. These Sundays highlighted the biblical calls to welcome refugees and modern stories of refugees in need. That's a potent religious message that's also a potent political message.

We need more prophetic preaching like that. When politicians demonize Muslims, Mexicans, or anyone else, we need to preach the importance of loving our neighbors. When politicians urge violence and torture, we need to preach the importance of loving our enemies. We don't need to mention candidates. But we do need to help Christians think first about these issues through the lens of the politics of Jesus. If many Christians are allowing party to trump principles, it might be because we've done a poor job of teaching the principles of the Kingdom. If people don't get the political messages of the Bible, then perhaps it's because we've ignored them to instead offer a watered-down story about nothing more than finding inner peace. We need more curriculum for Sunday School classes and small group Bible studies that help us process today's news events and political rhetoric from a biblical perspective.

An example of what we need more of is a great film on immigration called *Gospel Without Borders* created a few years ago by *Ethics Daily*. It explores biblical teachings about immigration and current myths about undocumented immigrants in the United States. Both Clinton and Trump—as well as President Barack Obama and many other politicians in both major parties—frequently repeat some of the myths as if factual. We screened the film with an ecumenical panel of Christian leaders at a church next to the Democratic convention in 2012, inviting delegates to walk over to learn more about this important topic and hear faith leaders offer perspectives challenging the delegates' own party leadership. Recognizing we cannot ignore the political sphere, we went to speak truth to power. It's a discussion needed even more today. The film includes segments that make it great for small groups to use. You can learn more at www.GospelWithoutBorders.net. We must not cloister ourselves while important moral and ethical debates rage around us.

5. Election Day Communion

One of the most impressive examples of the prophetic imagination we need came on election day in 2012. Nearly 900 churches and Christian organizations held a special communion service on that day, with services in all 50 states and Washington, D.C. Called

"Election Day Communion," two Mennonite pastors (one in Virginia and one in Indiana) and an Episcopalian lay author (in Michigan) launched the concept just three months before election day. And the idea quickly spread, even capturing attention in the *Washington Post*, *CNN*, *NPR*, and dozens of local newspapers and television stations. Churches from multiple denominations participated, with some services even jointly sponsored by multiple churches from different traditions. This nonpartisan effort sought to remind us where our first allegiance lies.

"On November 6, 2012, Election Day, we will exercise our right to choose," the initiative's website declared, "Some of us will choose to vote for Barack Obama. Some of us will choose to vote for Mitt Romney. Some of us will choose to vote for another candidate. Some of us will choose not to vote. ... But that evening while our nation turns its attention to the outcome of the presidential election, let's again choose differently. But this time, let's do it together. Let's meet at the same table, with the same host, to remember the same things."[12]

"We'll remember that real power in this world—the power to save, to transform, to change—ultimately rests not in political parties or presidents or protests but in the life, the death, and the resurrection of Jesus," the website added. "We'll remember that the only Christian nation in this world is the Church, a holy nation that crosses all human-made boundaries and borders. ... We'll remember that we do not conform to the patterns of this world, but we are transformed by the renewing of our minds (Romans 12:2). ... And we'll re-member the body of Christ as the body of Christ, confessing the ways in which partisan politics has separated us from one another and from God."[13]

It's a reminder that regardless who wins, Jesus is still King. It's a reminder that regardless the seemingly-important outcome, it's not the most important thing. It's a reminder that regardless of our disagreements on partisan politics, we are still to unite around a more important politics. I went to an Election Day Communion service at the church I attended at the time in Virginia. It started just as the polls closed, which forced me to focus on something other than the counting of ballots and the prognostications of pundits. As a political junkie, I kind of need a reminder to focus less on U.S. politics. That short service had no sermon, but included several songs and Bible readings, times for prayer and private confession, and communion. I made stickers for my church that featured a communion cup with the words "I Communed!" on it. We passed them out to people at the close of the service, many of them placing them on their shirts next to their "I Voted" stickers. While many churches held services at the close of voting, some held them during the day. Others had communion elements out for people to stop by and partake as they could during the day. This even occurred at churches used as voting locations, which means someone could go vote and then walk down the hallway and take communion.

Election Day Communion seemed like a perfect response to the nastiness of the 2012 campaign. It offered a chance for churches to reclaim the political agenda and remind people what really matters. The 2016 campaign needs this response even more. So let's plan Election Day Communion services at our churches. Let's get far more than 900 involved. And let's advertise the service for a month beforehand. Mention it each Sunday during that month and in other communication your church puts out. That way, during the month when the presidential campaign will likely be at its most intense, we'll all be reminding people of a more important political commitment to make on November 8. Amen!

I made the "I Communed!" sticker for my church's Election Day Communion service.

I took this selfie later that night as I watched election results.

VOTE YOUR CONSCIENCE

Appendix 1: Casting My Vote (All Day)

(Note: This essay was originally published at www.BrianKaylor.com on August 6, 2014, which was the day after a primary election day. You can find the original piece here: http://www.briankaylor.com/2014/08/casting-my-vote-all-day.html)

I voted yesterday.

That's not unusual. I am nearly religious about voting, showing up anytime the voting booths are open! But yesterday brought a couple of new voting experiences for me. It marked the first time I voted since moving from Virginia back to Missouri. Voting seemed a bit weird because in Virginia I always had a good friend who volunteered as a poll worker. I missed seeing him and joking with him as he asked questions to verify my identity.

My son, who always goes with me when I vote, apparently missed seeing my friend as well. Last November, my son (then not even two years old) ran down the line of voters and gave Mike a big bear hug. This time he hugged no one, which is probably good since he didn't know anyone there!

Yesterday brought an even bigger change for me as a voter. This was the first time in my 15 years of voting that I walked into a church building to vote in a civil election. My precinct was located in a church's event center that's not actually attached to the church's sanctuary and main building—and did not include many obvious religious messages or symbols—but it still meant I entered a church to vote.

I have long felt uneasy about elections held in church buildings. I worry this could be a space that does not truly provide a safe civic space for some. A public school just down the street would seem a more appropriate space for a public election. I worry it might unduly influence elections. Research, in fact, shows that where people vote slightly impacts how they vote, with voting in churches making people more conservative[1] (but that's not why I'm opposed to the idea!). But most of all I worry this could help Christians think it's okay to mix church and state.

After working through my ballot, which seemed to include marking "no" a lot, I went to the machine to feed in my civic offering.

I then picked up my "I voted" sticker. In Virginia, my son usually got a "future voter" sticker. They didn't have such stickers at my precinct yesterday but he really wanted a sticker so I grabbed him an "I voted" sticker as well. He quickly put it on his Pooh Bear (who had, of course, gone to the voting booth with us) and proudly stated, "Pooh vote." We hadn't even left the polling room yet so I'm afraid that might start some voter fraud rumors (oh, bother).

As I left the church building with my son and the "I voted" Pooh Bear, I continued to wear my "I voted" sticker. I like to vote in the morning and wear the sticker around as my civic witness.

Wearing the sticker seemed appropriate since I voted all day.

We went to the grocery store and I cast several votes: fair trade bananas over the other ones, healthy cereal over the sugary ones, and so on. Throughout the day I voted by choosing to do some things and choosing not to do others. Perhaps I should wear the sticker each day to remind me. I can't actually wear it again because my son ate it—seriously, he ripped it off my shirt last night, ate it, and repeatedly said, "I eat daddy sticker vote." But wearing it again could have been a good reminder that we don't just vote in ballot boxes.

VOTE YOUR CONSCIENCE

As I scan the election results—some good, some bad—I must remember that my opportunities to vote continue again today. In that way perhaps it's almost appropriate to vote in a church building. Just as worship and faith must be more than what happens in a building on Sunday, politics and civic duty must be more than what happens in a building on Tuesday. Even as the campaign signs come down—until news ones come up for the next election—we must still live out our votes.

BRIAN KAYLOR

Appendix 2: Rejecting a 'Loser' Savior

(Note: This essay was originally published at www.BrianKaylor.com on March 25, 2016, which was 'good Friday.' You can find the original piece here: http://www.briankaylor.com/2016/03/rejecting-loser-savior.html*)*

As Jesus marched into Jerusalem on that first 'palm Sunday,' the crowd eagerly cheered. They longed for a strong leader, one who could finally make Israel great again.

"We don't win anymore," one man might have said to his neighbor in between shouts of "hosanna!" and waving of palm leaves. "We used to win with Moses and Joshua—I love Joshua—and Solomon and David—nobody's better than David. Now we lose all the time."

The crowd cheered and shouted for the new king, a new warrior. Then Jesus rode by on a donkey's colt.

"Wait, why isn't he riding on a war horse?" the second man may have asked back to his neighbor. "I expected something classy. A colt is a bit too low energy. You know what I mean? It's just terrible, worst kind you can imagine. Look, I just thought he'd try something terrific. Like a white stallion. Just beautiful, the best."

As the energetic crowd welcomed Jesus into the Jerusalem, they seemed to see change coming. They yearned for someone who could make deals and get things done. They wanted someone willing to kill the Romans and maybe even soldiers' family members. They wanted someone to rebuild Nehemiah's wall and keep our people safe from those people. Surely this Jesus could be that savior.

The dream of the crowd soon dissipated. Over the next couple of days, Jesus cleansed the temple, again insisted he must die, and surrendered nonviolently to those who came to arrest him. Rather than whip the crowd into a violent frenzy against those hated 'others,' he instead criticized the failures of his own people. Rather than prepare his followers for battle, he instead scolded one for wielding a sword.

So just five days after the crowd welcomed Jesus into Jerusalem, a mob chanted for his death. It's a chant that's echoed throughout the years: "crucify him," "lynch him," "waterboard him," "kill him."

As the tortured Jesus stood before the angry crowd on Friday, the people chose Jesus Barabbas (often just called "Barabbas," which means 'son of the father'). The options couldn't be clearer. What kind of savior did they want? What kind of revolution did they desire? The nonviolent, self-sacrificing love preached by Jesus the Son of God? Or the violent, hate-filled guerilla warfare practiced by Jesus son of the father? The one who sat still while being punched in the face or the one who promised to send the enemy off on stretchers or worse?

There might have been a few people pointing out the vulgarity and bigotry of Barabbas. But the anger of the mob quickly drowned out those dissenting voices. Who wants to hear about how love trumps hate when it's easier to just fight?

"He's not a messiah," someone in the crowd may have hissed about Jesus of Nazareth as the soldiers led the condemned man away. "I like people who aren't crucified."

"What a dummy that Jesus, so overrated," someone else might have responded with agreement. "Such a loser. We need a strong fighter to make Israel great again."

VOTE YOUR CONSCIENCE

BRIAN KAYLOR

Appendix 3: An Eye for an Eye Makes the Bible Blind

(Note: This essay was originally published by Red Letter Christians *on April 26, 2016. You can find the original piece here: http://www.redletterchristians.org/eye-eye-makes-bible-blind)*

The question of a 'flat Bible' dominated a Sunday School class I guest taught a few years ago. The group had been reading and discussing a book[1] I wrote and invited me to class during a trip I took to visit family. The book didn't raise issues about whether each part of the Bible should be considered equally inspired and authoritative (a flat reading of the Bible). But a Baptist college professor in the class jumped in that direction after learning I attended a Mennonite church at the time. He argued Mennonites wrongly put the words of Jesus ahead of other parts of scriptures instead of viewing all of the Bible as equal.

I didn't push the topic too strongly since I wanted to focus on the issues I'd been invited to teach. The quick answer I gave included a defense of reading the 'red letters' as more authoritative and important. They are mountain peaks far above the small hills and valleys elsewhere in the Bible. We should read the rest of the Bible through the lens of Jesus rather than reading Jesus through the lens of the rest of the Bible. I pointed to the 'Sermon on the Mount' where Jesus himself rejected the idea of a 'flat Bible.'

"You have heard that it was said ... but I tell you..."

The things his audience had heard said before are still in our Bibles as teachings in the Mosaic laws. Jesus didn't fully reject those teachings but instead expanded them. To say the Mosaic laws are equal with the teachings of Jesus is to ignore the very words Jesus spoke.

I hadn't thought of that Sunday School class for a couple of years. And then came Donald Trump. Asked about his favorite Bible verse, the Republican presidential frontrunner offered a surprising answer.

"Well, I think many," Trump said in his characteristic hem-haw manner. "I mean, when we get into the Bible, I think many, so many. And some people, look, an eye for an eye, you can almost say that. That's not a particularly nice thing. But you know, if you look at what's happening to our country, I mean, when you see what's going on with our country, how people are taking advantage of us, and how they scoff at us and laugh at us. ... And we have to be firm and have to be very strong. And we can learn a lot from the Bible, that I can tell you."[2]

It's a nearly unbelievable answer, almost as if *Saturday Night Live*'s Trump character uttered the words. Has Trump even read a Bible before? Did he start in Genesis and give up long before making it to Matthew? Did he really have no clue that Jesus literally repudiated the very verse Trump lifts up as the best moral guide?

Upon further reflection, I wonder if I should applaud Trump. For his honesty. Few—if any others—would name the 'eye for an eye' passage as a favorite Bible verse. Yet too often it seems we live as if it's our favorite. From cheering for war to backing the death penalty. From demanding 'tough on crime' policies to advocating for nuclear weapons. From endorsing torture to consuming violent entertainment and sports. We may say with our mouths that our favorite verse is John 3:16 or 1 Corinthians 13:4 or Philippians 4:13 or some other inspiring verse. But too often our actions and politics suggest we really admire the text about 'an eye for an eye.'

Only a 'flat Bible' perspective can justify living in such a blind way. Instead we must recognize that the 'red letters' of Jesus—especially in the 'Sermon on the Mount'—call us to another path. A path our fear-mongering politicians hope we'll ignore. A path that calls us to embrace radical grace and love and forgiveness. A path that remains much harder to follow than merely swinging for someone's eye.

Appendix 4: On the Jericho ... No, Wait ... Büdingen Road

(Note: This essay was originally published at www.BrianKaylor.com on April 4, 2016. You can find the original piece here: http://www.briankaylor.com/2016/04/on-jericho-no-wait-budingen-road.html)

Sometimes it seems we know the biblical stories so well we don't actually understand them. I find it too easy to sit on a nice padded pew in a stained-glass sanctuary and smile while the preacher reads a familiar biblical text. Then I can nod my head, thank the pastor on the way out the door, and act like nothing's different.

Perhaps no parable demonstrates this more than the one we usually call "the parable of the good Samaritan." Fortunately, some modern characters recently reenacted this parable on a road in Germany.

Stefan Jagsch, a member of the anti-immigrant National Democratic Party in Germany, crashed his car into a tree near Büdingen. An outspoken critic of Germany admitting refugees, he is part of a political party criticized as "neo-Nazi" and known for xenophobic rhetoric. Suffering two broken legs and facial lacerations, Jagsch soon found himself helped by a couple of "good Samaritans." In true biblical fashion, the helpers were the last people Jagsch would expect—or want. Two Syrian refugees pulled the seriously-injured man from the wrecked car and performed first aid.

As it turns out, we know the story of the "good Samaritan" so well we often miss the point. In our churches, when the pastor starts the story, we can elbow the person next to us and proudly whisper, "I bet the good guy is the Samaritan" even though we don't have a clue what a Samaritan is. But when Jesus started the story, no one in his Jewish audience expected the hero to be a Samaritan. When Jesus mentioned a man was badly beaten on the road from Jerusalem to Jericho, someone likely elbowed the person next to them and angrily whispered, "I bet he was attacked by one of those ... [fill-in-the-blank] ... Samaritans." But the word filled in was not "good."

As I watch politicians in Germany, the United States, and elsewhere pass laws to criminalize and punish refugees and others who are among the "least of these," I recognize the need for us to hear the parable of the good neighbor in our own context. If Jesus stood before us today, he wouldn't talk about Samaritans. The story would need a new twist to shock us in the end. Perhaps he would talk about Donald Trump being helped by an undocumented Mexican immigrant. Or perhaps he'd mention Ted Cruz being helped by an LGBT activist. Or perhaps the best version Jesus could give today would be about a far-right, hyper-nationalist, anti-refugee, neo-Nazi politician being helped by a Syrian refugee.

VOTE YOUR CONSCIENCE

Appendix 5: Fellow Citizens of God's Kingdom

(Note: This essay was originally published in the May 2016 issue of Churchnet *magazine. You can find the original piece here: https://www.joomag.com/mag/0734645001464119563?page=12)*

A few months ago, a presidential candidate attacked the faith of one of his opponents by claiming "not a lot of evangelicals come out of Cuba."[1] This kind of religious-based political attack hurts both democracy and religion (as I argued in my book[2] on religious rhetoric in presidential campaigns). The attack, which the candidate repeated numerous times, also remains simply false. It turns out, Cuba is a land with many evangelicals.

Having traveled to western and central Cuba in 2014 with a Churchnet delegation, I knew there were Baptists and other evangelicals on the island nation. However, the recent trip to eastern Cuba brought an abundance of more evidence. The Baptist community remained faithful despite multiple governments, various social and economic shifts, natural disasters, and even persecution. We met pastors who showed us church buildings the government had seized.

But those same pastors also showed us their current facilities that are packed to overflowing for worship services. Over the last twenty years, Baptists in the Convención Bautista de Cuba Oriental (Baptist Convention of Eastern Cuba, CBCO) have planted about 400 new churches and thousands of smaller home groups! It seems Baptists of Cuba could teach U.S. evangelicals about church planting. Many people remain unreached, but God is clearly alive and at work in Cuba.

During the trip, I had the privilege of preaching at Cuarta Iglesia Bautista (Fourth Baptist Church) of Santiago de Cuba for the midweek service. Focusing on Romans 12, one of my main two points was about how we are together the Body of Christ. I noted how Baptists in the U.S. and Cuba need to know each other, hear from each other, and learn to suffer and rejoice with each other. There's something unique about the Kingdom of God—it transcends borders and crosses walls. When I pledge allegiance to this Kingdom, I am casting my lot with my brothers and sisters in Cuba, Guatemala, and around the world. Jesus prayed we would be one. Paul preached we are equal. We can live no differently.

I look forward to the possibilities of partnering with Cuban Baptists. We have much to learn from each other. And we need each other. Osbel Gutiérrez Pila, president of the CBCO and pastor at Cuarta

Iglesia Bautista, expressed his gladness that relations between Christians in the two nations remained strong despite strained diplomatic relations.

"Even in the tough times, the relations between the brothers in Cuba and the U.S. never ceased," he said. "The government may have differences but the brothers and sisters don't."

That's the way it should be among citizens of the Kingdom. Despite political rhetoric to the contrary, evangelicals are found in Cuba. They remain a faithful witness in their communities, but much work remains. Many diplomatic and economic barriers have already melted away since my earlier Cuban visit just 18 months earlier. Doors are opening. I pray we will be faithful to the call.

VOTE YOUR CONSCIENCE

BRIAN KAYLOR

Appendix 6: Aylan Kurdi

(Note: This essay was originally published at www.BrianKaylor.com on September 3, 2015. You can find the original piece here: http://www.briankaylor.com/2015/09/aylan-kurdi.html)

I lay by my sleeping son and stare.

It sounds a bit stalkerish, and perhaps it is. I look at him and then back at this screen, hoping for words that make sense, hoping his peacefulness can heal my soul.

Before nap time I looked at the news. Perhaps it was a mistake, but I don't think so. Ignorance isn't really bliss, it's an excuse. Yet another story of desperate refugees from Syria dying when their boat capsized in the Mediterranean Sea.

Only this time a photo stopped my breath.[1]

A three-year-old boy, Aylan Kurdi, lying on his stomach on the shore, water lapping up at his face.

He's dressed in clothes not much different from what my three-year-old son wore today. Was he also wearing a red shirt because it's what his favorite stuffed buddy, Winnie-the-Pooh, wears? Did his dad also pick out the blue shorts since they look good with the shirt? Did he also recently get those shoes as hand-me-downs from a family friend?

I want to shout.

I want to close my eyes and hope it was a bad dream.

I listen as my son breathes in and out. I want to squeeze him, but I let him sleep. When he awakes he'll probably want to splash in a little swimming pool. For him, water is safe and fun.

Reading another story, I learn the boy's older brother and mother also drowned, but his father survived. I look around.

I can't imagine living in a land so dangerous that the wild sea is safer. I can't imagine hopping in an unstable boat with my son and hoping we make it across the sea. Yet many people are faced with that reality. They seek the small chance they can provide a better life for their kids.

Meanwhile, people who think they should be president of the United States are running around complaining about "anchor babies." Those candidates call themselves "pro-life," but they clearly just mean they are "anti-abortion." Someone who is pro-life doesn't demean precious children with such hateful rhetoric. These candidates gush about God, but it seems like just a political tactic.

Those same candidates want to build a wall to keep people out, many of whom are children traveling alone as they flee violence. Maybe we should even build two walls, a candidate suggested—one on the northern border in addition to a southern one. Maybe even a moat. Maybe even alligators, or hippos, or whatever it takes to keep those people out. Could we build a new Mediterranean Sea on the border to keep them out?

Hungarian Prime Minister Viktor Orban argued refugees must be kept out because they are mostly Muslim, and therefore threaten to destroy "Europe's own Christian values."[2] He's partially right. This is a test of Europe's Christianity ... and they are currently failing. As are we in the United States.

Walling off the country to protect its "Christian" identity and heritage is actually unchristian. To look away as small kids drown is what will destroy a nation's Christian identity and heritage. This is not some hypothetical political debate. We are talking about real people with real dreams, real hopes, real families. People like Aylan Kurdi.

BRIAN KAYLOR

Appendix 7: What Would Jesus of Valdosta Say to Donald Trump

(Note: This essay was originally published by Red Letter Christians *on March 3, 2016. You can find the original piece here:* http://www.redletterchristians.org/what-would-jesus-of-valdosta-say-to-donald-trump*)*

On Monday, Republican presidential frontrunner Donald Trump held one of his 'yuge' rallies in Valdosta, Ga. While most people outside the Peach State are likely not familiar with that city near the Florida border, it plays a significant a role in one of the most imaginative religious texts of the 20th Century. In it we may also find a prophetic warning against the politics of Trump.

Clarence Jordan, an excommunicated Southern Baptist prophet who played an important role in the creation of Habitat for Humanity and who cofounded an interracial Christian farming community in southwestern Georgia in 1942, created the *Cotton Patch Gospel* translation of the New Testament in the 1960s. Using his Ph.D. in New Testament Greek, Jordan created a Bible version that not only translated the language but also the geographical and time context.

Rather than someone from long ago in a culture far away, Jordan recast Jesus as a white preacher from Georgia in the middle of the 20th Century. No longer does Jesus hail from Nazareth, but Valdosta. Can anything good come from such an insignificant place as that?

The beauty of Jordan's *Cotton Patch Gospel* comes in his brutal proximity. We can easily cheer Jesus criticizing the Pharisees and we can happily praise the 'good Samaritan' even if we have no clue who the Pharisees or Samaritans were in reality. But when Jordan's coreligionists read his translation, they found Jesus attacking white Protestant churchgoers instead of Pharisees. They also found a story of a man beaten up on the road from Atlanta to Albany who is helped by a black man after a white preacher and white gospel music leader left him for dead. That's the type of preaching that got Jesus crucified, or—as Jordan cast it—lynched. And Jordan's opponents reacted similarly by raining hellfire of machine gun bullets and dynamite blasts on his Koinonia Farm community.

I'm sure Trump knows nothing of the *Cotton Patch Gospel* (or that he should call its book 'Second Letter to the Atlanta Christians' instead of 'Two Letter to the Atlanta Christians'). However, as I listen to his speeches attacking Mexican immigrants, Muslims and other people—and especially as I see him winning the most votes from evangelicals—I recognize the great need for Jesus of Valdosta. Our ability to segregate our faith teachings on Sunday from our politics on Tuesday poses a serious threat to the credibility of our witness.

So I'd love to imagine what would have happened if Jesus of Valdosta had showed up to Trump's rally on Monday. If he somehow got through the security despite looking a bit like a Bernie Sanders supporter, I doubt he would've lasted long. He probably would've said something about how we should love immigrants and Muslims. He definitely would've stood in solidarity with the black students who were removed from the rally on their own college campus merely for being black. Before long, security would've dragged Jesus of Valdosta out as well while Trump bragged about wanting to "punch him in the face" to the cheers of the crowd.

Outside the rally, perhaps Jesus of Valdosta would've given a little sermon for interested onlookers. Maybe he would've talked about the need to build bridges instead of walls, or how we should be humble and self-sacrificing. Or maybe he would've mentioned how years ago his parents fled with him to Mexico to avoid persecution from a corrupt political leader. Or perhaps he would've repeated his first sermon, the one in the fourth chapter of Luke that he gave at a church in Valdosta:

The Lord's spirit is on me;

He has ordained me to break the good news to the poor people.

He has sent me to proclaim freedom for the oppressed.

And sight for the blind,

To help those who have been grievously insulted to find dignity;

To proclaim the Lord's new era.

And then perhaps like the crowd at the church when Jesus of Valdosta preached those words, those at the Trump rally would've attempted to grab him and kill him. But they probably wouldn't have tried crucifixion or lynching. Instead they'd probably hope President Trump would send that traitorous preacher to Guantanamo to be tortured with waterboarding and "a hell of a lot worse."

Perhaps this all sounds a bit silly, but do we really think Jesus of Nazareth would sit idly by as a womanizing and vulgar demagogue grabbed power by preaching hate against anyone who looked different? If we do, then perhaps that shows Jordan rightly recognized how the distance of time and space makes it possible to study the Bible on Sunday and then walk out the doors and make no connection to our own context. With so many white evangelicals lining up to cheer and vote for Trump, it seems we have domesticized and spiritualized Jesus of Nazareth. So perhaps we once again need Jesus of Valdosta. Or perhaps even better, we need Jesus of Ciudad Juárez or Jesus of Santiago de Cuba.

VOTE YOUR CONSCIENCE

About the Author

Dr. Brian Kaylor is an award-winning author, journalist, and speaker. He is also a (non-award-winning) stay-at-home dad. Brian's parents tell their friends he is like a Christian version of Castle (from the hit TV show) since he spends his time as a writer and dad. Brian assumes his parents also mention he and Castle are both witty and ruggedly handsome.

Brian is the author of three books on religion, politics, and communication: *Sacramental Politics: Religious Worship as Political Action* (Peter Lang, 2015), *Presidential Campaign Rhetoric in an Age of Confessional Politics* (Lexington Books, 2011) and *For God's Sake, Shut Up!* (Smyth & Helwys, 2007). Brian serves as the Generational Engagement Team Leader for Churchnet and Contributing Editor for *Ethics Daily*. He has a Ph.D. and an M.A. in Communication from the University of Missouri, and a B.A. in Communication and Christian Ministry from Southwest Baptist University. He and his wife, Jennifer, were married in June of 2004 and have a son.

VOTE YOUR CONSCIENCE

Learn more at www.BrianKaylor.com. You can follow Brian on Twitter: @BrianKaylor. You can find him on Instagram: @BrianKaylor. And you can like his author page on Facebook to keep up with his latest writings: www.facebook.com/BrianTKaylor

Brian Kaylor speaking at the 2016 Baptist World Alliance meeting in Vancouver.

(photo by Cliff Vaughn, *Ethics Daily*)

Acknowledgments

A famous author declared, "no man is an island." When it comes to authors, that's particularly true. No work comes from just one mind. I am thankful for the encouragement, insights, and critiques I received from several people as I worked on this book (though they didn't always know I was testing out book arguments on them). I'm thankful for Beau Underwood, Doyle Sager, Jim Hill, Nate Earley, my parents (Doug and Carol Kaylor), and my in-laws (John and Ronda Credille). And I'm especially appreciative of my wife, Jennifer. Don't blame any of them, however, for what you read. I didn't always take their advice. Any mistakes or bad arguments are fully my own (or the fault of my four-year-old son for distracting me).

I'm also thankful for those who've given me platforms to write about religion and politics during this campaign (including some of the pieces that appear in this book): Robert Parham and Zach Dawes at *Ethics Daily*, Bill Webb at *Word&Way*, Jonathan Wilson-Hartgrove at *Red Letter Christians*, Sarah Pulliam Bailey and Michelle Boorstein at *Washington Post*, and Catherine Woodiwiss at *Sojourners*. Their feedback—and the encouragement I've received from friends on Facebook and Twitter—helped propel me through this book.

VOTE YOUR CONSCIENCE

Endnotes

[1] See video here: http://video.foxnews.com/v/4879512783001
[2] Ibid.
[3] Numbers 15:39 (NIV)
[4] Proverbs 28:26 (NASB)
[5] Mark 8:36 (NRSV)
[6] Brian T. Kaylor, *Presidential campaign rhetoric in an age of confessional politics* (Lanham, MD: Lexington Books, 2011).
[7] Shane Claiborne and Chris Haw, *Jesus for President: Politics for ordinary radicals* (Grand Rapids, MI: Zondervan, 2008), 20.
[8] Thomas Jefferson, *Letter to the Danbury Baptists* (January 1, 1802), https://www.loc.gov/loc/lcib/9806/danpre.html
[9] Alexis Levinson, "Ted Cruz burns it down," *National Review* (July 21, 2016), http://www.nationalreview.com/corner/438163/ted-cruz-burns-it-down
[10] Richard Norton Smith, "Nelson Rockefeller's last stand," *Politico* (October 21, 2014), http://www.politico.com/magazine/story/2014/10/nelson-rockefellers-last-stand-112072
[11] Harry Enten, "Americans' distaste for both Trump and Clinton is record-breaking," *FiveThirtyEight* (May 5, 2016), http://fivethirtyeight.com/features/americans-distaste-for-both-trump-and-clinton-is-record-breaking
[12] Ibid.
[13] Michael Gerson, "The party of Lincoln is dying," *Washington Post* (June 9, 2016), https://www.washingtonpost.com/opinions/the-party-of-lincoln-is-dying/2016/06/09/e669380a-2e6b-11e6-9de3-6e6e7a14000c_story.html
[14] Ibid.
[15] Ecclesiastes 7:10 (NASB).
[16] Charles Marsh, *Wayward Christian soldiers: Freeing the gospel from political captivity* (Oxford, UK: Oxford University Press, 2007), 76.
[17] Ibid, 95.
[1] Eugene Kiely, "IG report on Clinton's emails," *FactCheck* (May 27, 2106), http://www.factcheck.org/2016/05/ig-report-on-clintons-emails
[2] Lauren Carroll, "FBI findings tear holes in Hillary Clinton's email defense," *PolitiFact* (July 6, 2016), http://www.politifact.com/truth-o-meter/statements/2016/jul/06/hillary-clinton/fbi-findings-tear-holes-hillary-clintons-email-def
[3] Find the full report here: https://oig.state.gov/system/files/esp-16-

03.pdf
[4] See his remarks here: https://www.fbi.gov/news/pressrel/press-releases/statement-by-fbi-director-james-b.-comey-on-the-investigation-of-secretary-hillary-clintons-use-of-a-personal-e-mail-system
[5] Watch the full hearing here: https://oversight.house.gov/hearing/oversight-state-department
[6] 1 Timothy 6:10 (NIV).
[7] Proverbs 28:15 (NIV).
[8] Proverbs 29:4 (NIV).
[9] Jo Becker and Mike McIntire, "Cash flowed to Clinton Foundation amid Russian uranium deal," *New York Times* (April 23, 2015), http://www.nytimes.com/2015/04/24/us/cash-flowed-to-clinton-foundation-as-russians-pressed-for-control-of-uranium-company.html
[10] David Sirota and Andrew Perez, "Clinton Foundation donors got weapons deals from Hillary Clinton's State Department," *International Business Times* (May 26, 2015), http://www.ibtimes.com/clinton-foundation-donors-got-weapons-deals-hillary-clintons-state-department-1934187
[11] Ibid.
[12] Joseph Cardinal Bernardin, *Consistent ethic of life conference address* (October 4, 1986), http://www.priestsforlife.org/magisterium/bernardinportland.html
[13] Ibid.
[14] See her campaign website: https://www.hillaryclinton.com/issues/womens-rights-and-opportunity
[15] Shane Claiborne, *Executing grace: how the death penalty killed Jesus and why it's killing us* (New York, NY: HarperOne, 2016).
[16] Jo Becker and Scott Shane, "Hillary Clinton, 'smart power' and a dictator's fall," *New York Times* (February 27, 2106), http://www.nytimes.com/2016/02/28/us/politics/hillary-clinton-libya.html
[17] Mark Landler, "How Hillary Clinton became a hawk," *New York Times* (April 21, 2016), http://www.nytimes.com/2016/04/24/magazine/how-hillary-clinton-became-a-hawk.html
[18] Juan Gonzalez, "Hillary Clinton's policy was a Latin American crime story," *New York Daily News* (April 12, 2016), http://www.nydailynews.com/news/national/gonzalez-clinton-policy-latin-american-crime-story-article-1.2598456
[19] James 3:6 (NIV).
[20] James 3:9-12 (NIV).

[21] Find a detailed list with audio clips here: Andrew Kaczynski and Nathan McDermott, "Donald Trump said a lot of gross things about women on 'Howard Stern,'" *BuzzFeed* (February 24, 2016), https://www.buzzfeed.com/andrewkaczynski/donald-trump-said-a-lot-of-gross-things-about-women-on-howar

[22] For examples in the rest of this paragraph (and more like them), see Nina Bahadur, "18 real things Donald Trump has actually said about women," *Huffington Post* (August 19, 2015), http://www.huffingtonpost.com/entry/18-real-things-donald-trump-has-said-about-women_us_55d356a8e4b07addcb442023

[23] See photo here: https://twitter.com/JerryJrFalwell/status/745325187776811008

[24] Ben Howe, "Here's what Donald Trump said about Jesus in that Playboy mag that Jerry Falwell Jr. posed in front of," *RedState* (June 22, 2016), http://www.redstate.com/aglanon/2016/06/22/heres-donald-trump-said-jesus-playboy-mag-jerry-falwell-posed-front

[25] Ibid.

[26] Ibid.

[27] Neetzan Zimmerman, "Trump mocks Fiorina's physical appearance: 'Look at that face!'" *The Hill* (September 9, 2015), http://thehill.com/blogs/blog-briefing-room/253178-trump-insults-fiorinas-physical-appearance-look-at-that-face

[28] Galatians 3:28 (NIV).

[29] Max Lucado, "Trump doesn't pass the decency test," *Washington Post* (February 26, 2016), https://www.washingtonpost.com/posteverything/wp/2016/02/26/max-lucado-trump-doesnt-pass-the-decency-test

[30] Ibid.

[31] Brent Walker, *Testimony* (June 8, 2004), http://www.judiciary.senate.gov/imo/media/doc/walker_testimony_06_08_04.pdf

[32] Leonardo Blair, "Trump mocks Carson's Christian conversion, calls him scary pathological enigma," *Christian Post* (November 13, 2015), http://www.christianpost.com/news/trump-mocks-carsons-christian-conversion-calls-him-scary-pathological-enigma-149971

[33] Ibid.

[34] Daniel Burke, "What Seven-day Adventists like Ben Carson believe," *CNN* (November 4, 2015), http://www.cnn.com/2015/10/27/politics/seventh-day-adventist-beliefs

[35] See video here: https://youtu.be/8Xo78F_yKc4

[36] Ibid.

[37] Ashley Killough, "Trump: 'We don't know anything about Hillary in

terms of religion,'" *CNN* (June 21, 2016), http://www.cnn.com/2016/06/21/politics/donald-trump-hillary-clinton-religion

[38] Engy Abdelkader, *When Islamophobia turns violent: The 2016 U.S. presidential elections* (Washington, D.C.: Prince Alwaleed Bin Talal Center for Muslim-Christian Understanding at Georgetown University, 2016), http://bridge.georgetown.edu/wp-content/uploads/2016/05/When-Islamophobia-Turns-Violent.pdf

[39] Russell Moore, "Is Donald Trump right about closing the border to Muslims?" (December 7, 2105), http://www.russellmoore.com/2015/12/07/is-donald-trump-right-about-closing-the-border-to-muslims

[40] Jon Ward, "Former Rubio advisor holds homemade anti-Trump sign outside evangelical meeting," *Yahoo News* (June 21, 2016), https://www.yahoo.com/news/former-rubio-adviser-holds-homemade-000000082.html

[41] Ibid.

[42] Matthew 5:9 (NIV).

[43] Watch these and other examples here: http://www.nytimes.com/video/us/100000004269364/trump-and-violence.html

[44] John McCain, "Bin Laden's death and the debate over torture," *Washington Post* (May 11, 2011), https://www.washingtonpost.com/opinions/bin-ladens-death-and-the-debate-over-torture/2011/05/11/AFd1mdsG_story.html

[45] Ibid.

[46] Find the debate transcript here: https://www.washingtonpost.com/opinions/bin-ladens-death-and-the-debate-over-torture/2011/05/11/AFd1mdsG_story.html

[47] Steve Guest, "Trump on waterboarding: 'I love it, I think it's great,'" *Daily Caller* (April 20, 2106), http://dailycaller.com/2016/04/20/trump-on-waterboarding-i-love-it-i-think-its-great-video

[48] Tom LoBianco, "Donald Trump on terrorists: 'Take out their families,'" *CNN* (December 3, 2015), http://www.cnn.com/2015/12/02/politics/donald-trump-terrorists-families

[49] Ali Vitali, "Donald Trump on terror: You have to 'fight fire with fire,'" *NBC News* (June 28, 2016), http://www.nbcnews.com/politics/2016-election/donald-trump-terror-you-have-fight-fire-fire-n600771

[50] LoBianco.

[51] Martin Luther King, Jr., *Strength to love* (Minneapolis, MN: Fortress

Press), p. 47.
[52] Matthew MacWilliams, "The one weird trait that predicts whether you're a Trump supporter," *Politico* (January 17, 2016), http://www.politico.com/magazine/story/2016/01/donald-trump-2016-authoritarian-213533
[53] Ibid.
[54] Michael Gryboski, "Donald Trump supporters display 'authoritarian personality,' psychologists say," *Christian Post* (March 12, 2016), http://www.christianpost.com/news/donald-trump-supporters-display-authoritarian-personality-psychologists-say-159098
[55] Ibid.
[56] Audie Cornish, "Why do evangelicals support Donald Trump? A pastor explains," *NPR* (February 25, 2016), http://www.npr.org/2016/02/25/468149440/why-do-evangelicals-support-donald-trump-a-pastor-explains.
[57] Listen to Mike Gallager's July 12, 2016 radio interview with Robert Jeffress here: http://www.mikeonline.com/dr-robertjeffress-peter_wehner-join-mike-for-an-important-debate-over-evangelical-christians-support-of-trump
[58] Mark Hensch, "Billy Graham's son: 'I have no hope' in either party's candidates," *The Hill* (March 9, 2016), http://thehill.com/blogs/ballot-box/presidential-races/272398-billy-grahams-son-i-have-no-hope-in-gop-or-dem-fields
[59] David Brody, "Donald Trump as King David?" *CBN News* (March 14, 2016), http://www1.cbn.com/thebrodyfile/archive/2016/03/14/donald-trump-as-king-david
[60] 1 Samuel 8:6, 19-20 (NIV).
[61] Ward.
[62] See video here: http://www.usatoday.com/videos/news/nation/2016/01/18/78967780
[63] Find speech transcript here: http://time.com/3923128/donald-trump-announcement-speech
[64] Ibid.
[65] Jay Hathaway, "More than half of Trump's retweets are white supremacists praising him," *New York* (January 27, 2016), http://nymag.com/selectall/2016/01/donald-trump-mostly-retweets-white-supremacists.html
[66] See ad here: https://youtu.be/qCQhBYEMRQI
[67] Randall Balmer, "Trump's success with evangelical voters isn't surprising. It was inevitable," *Washington Post* (May 16, 2016), https://www.washingtonpost.com/posteverything/wp/2016/05/16/trump

s-success-with-evangelical-voters-isnt-surprising-it-was-inevitable
⁶⁸ Michael Gerson, "The most depressing moment of the 2016 race," *Washington Post* (May 30, 206), https://www.washingtonpost.com/opinions/the-most-depressing-moment-of-2016/2016/05/30/bdb1807a-2457-11e6-aa84-42391ba52c91_story.html

Endnotes for Chapter 3
¹ Brian T. Kaylor, *Presidential campaign rhetoric in an age of confessional politics* (Lanham, MD: Lexington Books, 2011).
² Parts of my article on Trump are used in this section. For the original, see: Brian Kaylor, "Religious conservatives cheer Trump at conference," *Ethics Daily* (June 6, 2011), http://www.ethicsdaily.com/religious-conservatives-cheer-trump-at-conference-cms-18007
³ See a video of that moment here: https://youtu.be/yKr9sr9xKK8
⁴ Hillary Clinton, *Remarks at Baptist convention in Atlanta* (January 31, 2008), http://www.presidency.ucsb.edu/ws/index.php?pid=77089
⁵ Brian Kaylor, "Church attendance as antidote to Donald Trump," *Ethics Daily* (March 1, 2016), http://www.ethicsdaily.com/church-attendance-as-antidote-to-donald-trump-cms-23283
⁶ Ibid.
⁷ W. Scott Lamb, *Huckabee: The authorized biography* (Nashville, TN: W Publishing, 2015).
⁸ Brian Kaylor, "Evangelicals in Middle America less supportive of Trump," *Ethics Daily* (March 4, 2016), http://www.ethicsdaily.com/evangelicals-in-middle-america-less-supportive-of-trump-cms-23294
⁹ Harold F. Bass, Jr., *Historical dictionary of United States political parties* (Lanham, MD: Scarecrow Press, 2009).
¹⁰ Kaylor, "Evangelicals in Middle America less supportive of Trump."
¹¹ Ibid.
¹² Ibid.
¹³ Brandon Ambrosino, "A tale of two Falwell brothers," *Politico* (July 21, 2016), http://www.politico.com/magazine/story/2016/07/jerry-falwell-jonathan-gop-convention-trump-evangelical-conservative-christians-214082
¹⁴ Russell Moore, "Why this election makes me hate the word 'evangelical,'" *Washington Post* (February 29, 2016), https://www.washingtonpost.com/news/acts-of-faith/wp/2016/02/29/russell-moore-why-this-election-makes-me-hate-the-word-evangelical

[15] Ibid.
[16] See: Brian Kaylor, "Franklin Graham espouses debunked 'birther' claims," *Ethics Daily* (April 27, 2011), http://www.ethicsdaily.com/franklin-graham-espouses-debunked-birther-claims-cms-17813
[17] David Gibson, "Southern Baptist leader: Donald Trump a 'lost' soul who must repent," *Religion News Service* (June 5, 206), http://religionnews.com/2016/06/05/southern-baptist-leader-donald-trump-a-lost-soul-who-must-repent
[18] Eugene Scott, "Trump believes in God, but hasn't sought forgiveness," *CNN* (July 18, 2015), http://www.cnn.com/2015/07/18/politics/trump-has-never-sought-forgiveness
[19] Ibid.
[20] Cal Thomas, "Trump interview—The transcript," *Tribune Content Agency* (June 8, 2016), http://calthomas.com/node/985
[21] Ibid.
[22] Ibid.
[23] Ibid.
[24] Matthew 16:16 (NIV).
[25] 1 Timothy 6:5 (NIV).
[26] 1 Timothy 6:7-10 (NIV).
[27] See Falwell's introduction and Trump's speech here: https://youtu.be/xSAyOlQuVX4
[28] "Evangelicals and Donald Trump," *Religion & Ethics Newsweekly* (June 17, 2106), http://www.pbs.org/wnet/religionandethics/2016/06/17/evangelicals-donald-trump/30959
[29] Michelle Boorstein and Julie Zauzmer, "Thrilling Christian conservative audience, Trump vows to lift ban on politicking, appoint antiabortion judges," *Washington Post* (June 22, 2016), https://www.washingtonpost.com/news/acts-of-faith/wp/2016/06/20/how-can-trump-win-the-many-undecided-evangelicals-we-asked-them
[30] Emily McFarlan Miller, "Is Donald Trump now a born-again Christian?" *Religion News Service* (June 25, 2016), http://religionnews.com/2016/06/25/is-donald-trump-now-a-born-again-christian
[31] Proverbs 23:1-3 (NIV).

Endnotes for Chapter 4
[1] Robert D. Putnam and David E. Campbell, *American grace: How*

religion divides and unites us (New York, NY: Simeon & Schuster, 2010).
[2] Robert D. Putnam and David E. Campbell, "Walking away from church," *Los Angeles Times* (October 17, 2010), http://articles.latimes.com/2010/oct/17/opinion/la-oe-1017-putnam-religion-20101017
[3] Ibid.
[4] Ibid.
[5] Ibid.
[6] John Danforth, *Faith and politics: How the "moral values debate divides America and how to move forward together* (New York, NY: Penguin Books, 2006), 213.
[7] Brian T. Kaylor, *Presidential campaign rhetoric in an age of confessional politics,* (Lanham, MD: Lexington Books, 2011).
[8] Jeremiah 6:13-15 (NIV)
[9] Kaylor, *Presidential campaign rhetoric in an age of confessional politics.*
[10] John F. Kennedy, *Address to the Greater Houston Ministerial Alliance* (September 12, 1960), http://www.jfklibrary.org/Asset-Viewer/ALL6YEBJMEKYGMCntnSCvg.aspx
[11] Ibid.
[12] David Kuo, *Tempting faith: An inside story of political seduction* (New York, NY: Free Press, 2006), 61, emphasis in original.
[13] Tony Campolo, *Red letter Christians: A citizen's guide to faith & politics* (Ventura, CA: Regal, 2008), 36.
[14] Ibid, 37.
[15] Laurie Goodstein, "Religious Right, frustrated, trying new tactic on G.O.P.," *New York Times* (March 23, 1998), http://www.nytimes.com/1998/03/23/us/religious-right-frustrated-trying-new-tactic-on-gop.html?src=pm
[16] Gary Bauer, "Kudos to Ted Cruz," *The Pulse 2016* (May 5, 2016), http://thepulse2016.com/gary-bauer/2016/05/05/kudos-to-ted-cruz
[17] Goodstein.
[18] Jeremiah 3:16 (NIV).
[19] Isaiah 1:21 (NIV).
[20] Psalm 106:39 (NIV).
[21] Hosea 9:1 (NIV).
[22] Ezekiel 16:16, 32-34 (NIV).
[23] Todd Starnes, "Should Christians vote for Donald Trump," *Fox News* (May 12, 2016), http://www.foxnews.com/opinion/2016/05/12/should-christians-vote-for-donald-trump.html
[24] Michelle Singer, "Rudy Giuliani: Relationships vs. resume," *CBS*

News (August 21, 2007), http://www.cbsnews.com/news/rudy-giuliani-relationships-vs-resume
²⁵ Arian Campo-Flores, "Christian conservatives can't find a candidate," *Newsweek* (December 9, 2010), http://www.newsweek.com/christian-conservatives-cant-find-candidate-68945
²⁶ Elizabeth Dias, "Inside Donald Trump's private meeting with evangelicals," *Time* (June 20, 2016), http://time.com/4375975/donald-trump-evangelical-conservative-leaders-meeting

Endnotes for Chapter 5
¹ K. Allan Blume, "Pasto'rs plan to raise the Christian flag," *Baptist Press* (July 6, 2015), http://www.bpnews.net/45089/pastors-plan-to-raise-the-christian-flag
² Ibid.
³ John Boyle, "Should Christian flat trump American flag," *Asheville Citizen-Times* (December 2, 2015), http://www.citizen-times.com/story/news/local/2015/12/02/answer-man-should-christian-flag-trump-american-flag-church/76658020
⁴ You can see the prayer here: https://youtu.be/a3sQ1JuOvhk
⁵ Brian Kaylor, *Sacramental politics: Religious worship as political action* (New York, NY: Peter Lang Publishing, 2015).
⁶ Erwin R. Stutzman, *From nonresistance to justice: The transformation of Mennonite Church peace rhetoric, 1908-2008* (Scottdale, PA: Herald Press, 2011), 292.
⁷ Ben Irwin, "In 24 hours" (November 5, 2012), http://electiondaycommunion.org/2012/11/05/in-24-hours
⁸ William T. Cavanaugh, *Theopolitical imagination: Discovering the liturgy as a political act in an age of global consumerism* (Edinburgh, Scotland: T. & T. Clark, 2002), 42.
⁹ Ibid, 50.
¹⁰ Brian Kaylor, *Sacramental politics: Religious worship as political action* (New York, NY: Peter Lang Publishing, 2015).
¹¹ https://www.facebook.com/BorderChurch.
¹² Mark 10:9 (KJ).
¹³ Shane Claiborne and Chris Haw, *Jesus for president: Politics for ordinary radicals* (Grand Rapids, MI: Zondervan, 2008), 39-40.
¹⁴ Leviticus 19:33-34 (CEB).
¹⁵ Deuteronomy 10:18-19 (CEB).
¹⁶ Psalm 146:9 (CEB).
¹⁷ "Concerns about Dr. Ben Carson's invitation to the SBC Pastor's Conference," *Baptist21* (April 23, 2015), http://baptist21.com/blog-

posts/2015/concerns-about-dr-ben-carsons-invitation-to-the-sbc-pastors-conference

[18] Ibid.

[19] Thomas Kidd, "'Theological police'? Paleo evangelicals and Ben Carson," *Patheos* (May 5, 2015), http://www.patheos.com/blogs/anxiousbench/2015/05/paleo-evangelicals-and-ben-carson

Endnotes for Chapter 6

[1] Mark Martin, "Anne Graham Lotz on who she'll support in the 2016 election, *CBN* (May 12, 2016), http://www1.cbn.com/cbnnews/us/2016/may/anne-graham-lotz-on-who-shell-support-in-the-2016-election

[2] Ibid.

[3] Ibid.

[4] Michael Gerson, "Evangelicals must not bear the mark of Trump," *Washington Post* (June 2, 2016), https://www.washingtonpost.com/opinions/evangelicals-may-carry-the-mark-of-trump/2016/06/02/dc0f59b4-28eb-11e6-ae4a-3cdd5fe74204_story.html

[5] Matthew 4:8-9 (NIV).

[6] Gerson.

[7] Ibid.

[8] Ibid.

[9] Ibid.

[10] Ibid.

[11] http://www.ptsem.edu/Library/index.aspx?menu1_id=6907&menu2_id=6904&id=8450

[12] http://electiondaycommunion.org

[13] Ibid.

Endnote for Appendix 1

[1] Abraham M. Rutchick, "Deus ex machina: The influence of polling place on voting behavior," *Political Psychology* 31 (2010), 209-225.

Endnotes for Appendix 3

[1] Brian Kaylor, *For God's sake, shut up!: Lessons for Christians on how to speak effectively and when to remain silent* (Macon, GA: Smyth & Helwys, 2007).

[2] Hear Trump's interview here: http://wham1180.iheart.com/onair/bob-lonsberry-3440/bob-lonsberry-talks-with-donald-trump-14604930/

Endnotes for Appendix 5
[1] Theodore Schleifer, "Donald Trump launches first attacks against Ted Cruz," *CNN* (December 12, 2015), http://www.cnn.com/2015/12/11/politics/donald-trump-ted-cruz-iowa-ethanol
[2] Brian T. Kaylor, *Presidential campaign rhetoric in an age of confessional politics* (Lanham, MD: Lexington Books, 2011).

Endnotes for Appendix 6
[1] See the photos here: http://www.theguardian.com/world/2015/sep/02/shocking-image-of-drowned-syrian-boy-shows-tragic-plight-of-refugees
[2] Rick Noack, "Muslims threaten Europe's Christian identity, Hungary's leader says," *Washington Post* (September 3, 2015), https://www.washingtonpost.com/news/worldviews/wp/2015/09/03/muslims-threaten-europes-christian-identity-hungarys-leader-says

www.ingramcontent.com/pod-product-compliance
Lightning Source LLC
Chambersburg PA
CBHW071452040426
42444CB00008B/1311